Arabella Boxer

This unmistakable spice is shaped like a star
and has a strong smell of aniseed mixed
with licorice.

The Spice Book

The nutmeg kernel is oval in shape ... it has a hard, brown, uneven surface and a paler interior.

The Spice Book

Arabella Boxer

photography by Sandra Lane

THUNDER BAY
P·R·E·S·S

Saffron is made from the dried stigmas of a species of crocus.

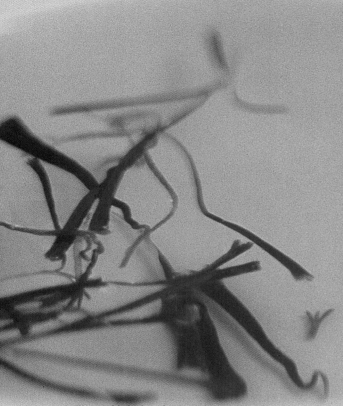

First published in the United States by Thunder Bay Press, 1997

Thunder Bay Press
5880 Oberlin Drive, Suite 400
San Diego, CA 92121

First Published in Great Britain in 1997 by Hamlyn,
an imprint of Reed International Books Limited
Michelin House, 81 Fulham Road,
London, SW3 6RB

Main text set in 10 on 17 pt Linotype Sabon

ISBN 1-57145-094-7

Library of Congress Cataloging-in-Publication Data available upon request.

Produced by Mandarin Book Production

Printed and bound in Hong Kong

Publishing Director: Laura Bamford

Senior Editor: Sasha Judelson
Editor: Barbara Horn

Art Director: Keith Martin
Senior Designer: Louise Leffler

Photographer: Sandra Lane
Home Economist: Louise Pickford
Stylist: Wei Tang
Picture Research: Claire Gouldstone

Indexer: Ann Barrett

Production Controller: Dawn Mitchell

contents

introduction

We tend to think of spices as food flavorings, but in earlier times their uses were manifold. Some, like aniseed and fennel, were used as medicaments in the form of infusions, decoctions, and poultices; others, like turmeric, as dyes, or, like cinnamon, cloves, and licorice, as incense; still others, like ginger and saffron, were used in baths, or, like myrrh and sesame seeds, in cosmetics. Similarly, in those days the understanding of what could be used to flavor food was broader and more complex than it is today in many cultures.

In the eighth century, on his death, the Venerable Bede left to his fellow monks his collection of spices, which included aniseed, cinnamon, cloves, cumin, cardamom, galangal, ginger, and licorice. In addition to these there were others, whose names mean little to us now: gromic, pelletour, eryngo, gelofrus, and sucket. By the fifteenth century we find mention of other spices: saffron, sandalwood (called sanders), mace, and mustard. In the seventeenth century, after the formation of the East India Company, we read of pine nuts, candied citrus peel, and pickled broom buds being put to use in the kitchen. In the *Compleat City and Country Cook*, by Charles Carter, published in 1732, one of the recipes for icing a cake lists musk and amber among the ingredients. Both are animal secretions: musk comes from the male musk deer, and amber, or ambergris, is a product of the sperm whale, found floating in tropical seas. These are exotic items that I would not have expected to find in an eighteenth century kitchen; both were used primarily in perfumery, while musk also had a medicinal use as a stimulant and antispasmodic.

Sadly, the traditions of multiple spicing and seasoning have long been forgotten in many Western cuisines. For the past century people have tended to separate different ingredients into categories, and fairly narrow ones at that. Even within the context of food, spices have been denied their individual flexibility, wherein lies much of their appeal. In the United Kingdom, the use of nutmeg, for instance, has been limited to little more than flavoring bread sauce or sprinkling over a custard, while a combination of cinnamon, nutmeg, and cloves, called "pudding spice" or simply "mixed spice," has been considered adequate for every sweet dish. Likewise, a commercially produced curry powder was thought to be all that was required to produce a series of Indian dishes.

At the other end of the scale is the scene in a typical Indian kitchen, where much of each day is spent preparing spices, and where a mixture of different spices is roasted and ground for every dish. At least, that is how it used to be, and still is in rural areas, but in the cities more and more women are enlisting the aid of food processors and spice mills, even resorting to buying their spice mixtures.

Setting out to write a book on spices is a daunting enterprise, for no one person can possibly know all there is to know about each and every spice, and how it is used in every corner of the globe. There are over one hundred different species of chili growing in Mexico alone, for example, and many of these chilies have names that change from region to region.

I have tended to concentrate on the way spices are used in those areas of the world that I know reasonably well and have visited several times; possibly even written about. These include the Mediterranean, North Africa, the Middle East, and Japan. Single visits to India and China have not been enough to familiarize me with the use of spices there, so for these countries and for Southeast Asia, where I have never been, I have relied on the help of friends and colleagues, and visits to good authentic restaurants.

Unless one has a deep love for a particular country and a genuine desire to reproduce some of its dishes as accurately as possible, there seems little harm in adapting ideas from here and there. In any case, ethnic dishes never taste exactly as they do in their place of origin when transposed to another country, where the raw ingredients — even the water — are not quite the same. I remember how after a family holiday in a rented house in Morocco, where we had grown to love the coffee that we bought each week in Tangiers, we purchased an identical coffee pot and a supply of the same coffee to take home. But it never tasted the same; soon we went back to our old ways, brewing Santos and Java blend in a dented metal Neapolitan coffee pot.

Since the end of World War II a growing enthusiasm for international cuisine has spread and continues unabated. But this is confined largely to restaurant meals and the purchase of packaged, ready-to-eat dishes for reheating in the microwave. Thus, chicken tikka masala, sweet-and-sour pork, and chili con carne may have almost reached the status of national dishes while being freshly cooked in only a small number of our own kitchens. Many manufacturers now produce jars of cook-in sauces, cans of spiced beans, and bottles of salsa. These are bland approximations of the real thing; they may not be bad as far as they go, but they share that dreaded sameness that characterizes packaged foods. How much better, and more enjoyable, to buy the spices themselves, for these never change, and from that cook something yourself. It's certainly more rewarding, as well as cheaper, healthier, and more welcoming.

For the simplest of accompaniments or snacks, broil tomato halves until just blackened and then sprinkle with cracked black pepper and ground coriander.

In their fresh state, nutmeg kernels are closely covered by the bright-red mace casing.

Far left: Picking the pistils from the crocus sativus is a very delicate process. It must be done by hand; after that the saffron is extracted.

spice
directory

Anethum graveolens

dill seeds

Dill is grown primarily for the sake of its leaves, which are used fresh, as an herb; but in Russia, Scandinavia, and the United States the seeds are also prized. In Russia they are used mainly for pickling fish and vegetables, while in the Scandinavian countries they are added to potato dishes and used in baking rye bread. The dill pickles, so popular with pastrami and corned beef sandwiches in the United States, are made with small cucumbers pickled in vinegar flavored with dill seeds. In the U.S., the two forms of dill are differentiated by calling them dill weed (the leaf) and dill seed.

Dill is an annual, a native of the Mediterranean region and southern parts of Russia. It is very similar to fennel in appearance, but milder and more delicate in flavor. (Fennel and dill should not be grown in close proximity, as they will cross-pollinate and their flavors merge.) The yellow flowers are borne in umbels in midsummer, and the seeds should be left to ripen on the plant before harvesting and drying. They may then be used in the kitchen or be kept to sow the following spring.

celery seeds

Apium graveolens

Celery is a biennial and produces seed only in its second year. During the first year the stems and leaves may be used.

Celery seeds are a useful flavoring, good for adding to soups and stews, unless they already contain celery. The flavors of celery seeds and cabbage go well together; they are delicious in cole slaws and other cabbage salads, as well as potato salads. Celery seeds may also be used to season meat loaf and the crusts of meat pies.

Celery salt is the best seasoning for hard-boiled eggs. To make celery salt, pound 4 parts celery seed with 1 part sea salt in a mortar.

cayenne

Capsicum frutescens

Cayenne, or red pepper, is not related to black or white pepper, which is the fruit of a climbing vine. It is made from the dried and ground flesh and seeds of the fiercely hot bird (bird's eye) chili, which belongs to the same family as the mild red and green bell pepper, the capsicum. It is very similar, but not identical, to chili powder; it is usually slightly less hot in flavor.

Cayenne reached Great Britain from India in 1548, at a time when highly spiced food was at the peak of its appeal. Yet over 400 years later, cayenne has retained its popularity in the West, adding the required heat to curries and spreads, and to savory recipes such as Welsh rarebit and cheese straws.

paprika

Capsicum annuum

Paprika is made from mild varieties of capsicum, or bell pepper, which have had their seeds and inner membranes removed before being dried and ground. The capsicum grew wild in Mexico, where it was discovered and was then taken to Europe by the Spaniards in the first part of the sixteenth century.

Paprika was first made in Hungary, after the capsicum had been brought there by the Turks, and became highly popular; it is still used today to flavor many Hungarian dishes, particularly goulash. Spanish paprika, called *pimentón*, is slightly different from the Central European variety, being made from a different species of capsicum. In both Spain and Hungary, paprika is manufactured in several grades based on quality, strength — the hottest is almost comparable to chili powder — and price.

Paprika should be bought in small amounts and replaced often, for, even more than with other spices, both flavor and color deteriorate quickly. The best quality paprika is a bright red, which is one of its virtues; a dusty, blood-red paprika is probably stale.

chilies

Capsicum frutescens

Chilies grew first in the Amazon region of South America and in Mexico; tiny red berries with a fiery heat, they were much appreciated by the Indians. Even before the arrival of Christopher Columbus, chilies had spread northward to the southwest of North America, and eastward to the Caribbean. Columbus took them with him when he returned to Spain, and from there they reached Portugal. The Portuguese carried chilies with them to India when establishing their trading posts at Cochin.

The arrival of the chili revolutionized Indian cooking. Until then, the only sources of pungency, or "heat," had been the peppercorn and the mustard seed. The variety of chilies available in India has never been great; unlike Mexico, where there are over 100 varieties, India has only two or three species from which to choose. (China has only one species of chili.)

Chilies vary hugely and are often hard to identify, as Diana Kennedy, the acknowledged authority on Mexican food, explains in her book *The Cuisines of Mexico* (Harper & Row, 1986): "Chilies are air-pollinated and cross easily; the local names change from place to place; and some are grown in remote mountainous areas where climatic conditions can vary enormously within a few miles, producing

many different varieties." Even the few that we find in local stores vary in size, shape, color, and strength. Their degree of heat was measured in 1911 in Scoville units. Chilies range from the blandest, such as sweet bell peppers at 0 Scoville units, to the fiery habañero, at 300,000 Scoville units. (For convenience, a reduced heat scale ranging from 0/10 to 10/10 has been devised.) But the heat can vary within any one species, depending on the growing conditions. A hot climate increases heat, as does too little water, or too much — anything that causes stress in the plant.

The capsaicin, which is the heat-producing element, is contained in the inner membrane, the veins, and the seeds. Thus the heat content may be decreased by discarding the membrane and all, or at least some, of the seeds. In the case of dried chilies, the inner membrane has more or less vanished, and the seeds are easily shaken out and discarded.

On the whole, the hottest chilies are the tiny ones, such as the tabasco, cayenne, and bird or bird's eye. It is hard for some people, including me, to ignore the heat and learn to appreciate the flavor, although this is what is of prime importance to the Mexicans, who are probably the greatest exponents of chilies. I tend to settle for the middle range, 5 to 7 out of 10 on the heat scale, as the very hot habañero deadens my whole mouth, tongue, and throat. My current favorite is the chipotle, a smoke-dried jalapeño, 6 to 7 on the heat scale, with a delicious, subtle, smoky flavor.

Chilies are easily grown, but they are not frost resistant and cannot survive winter outdoors except in tropical and subtropical climates. Sow the seed under glass at the end of winter, then plant outside in late spring. The plants look lovely grown in large pots on the patio, or even in the house.

Dried peppers are easy to use. Simply cut off the stems and shake out the seeds, then break the pepper into pieces and cover it with a little almost-boiling water. Leave it for 15–20 minutes, then drain, reserving the water. Chop the chilies coarsely and put them in a small blender or electric

mill with half the soaking water and process to a purée. If using a hard-skinned, woody variety, such as cascabel, the purée may need to be strained. Alternatively, put the whole chilies in a small pan of cold water, bring to a boil, simmer for 5 minutes, then remove from the heat and leave for another 5 minutes. The chilies may also be steamed instead of simmered.

Chilies have an amazing effect on the whole system, and can clear the nasal passages and banish colds, apathy and mild depression. They are a forceful stimulant and, by electrifying the saliva glands and digestive juices, they aid the digestive process, especially of starches. For this reason Harissa (see page 59) is admirably paired with couscous. Chilies also stimulate the sweat glands, causing perspiration to flow and lowering the body temperature in case of fever, and can create a general feeling of well-being. But they must be used with caution, especially by those who are unaccustomed to their heat potential. An overdose of chili heat can damage the mucous membrane lining the mouth, nose, throat, stomach, and intestine. To relieve the burning sensation after eating too hot a chili, the best remedy is cold dairy food — ice cream, yogurt, milk — or bananas; do not drink beer. Be sure to wash your hands in warm, soapy water after handling chilies, and do not touch your eyes, lips, or sensitive skin before doing so. People with sensitive skin should wear rubber gloves when handling chilies to avoid the heat reaching their skin.

hot red pepper flakes
Capsicum frutescens

These are a marvelous shortcut for the busy cook who needs to spark up a bland dish. For those, like myself, who tend to fall back on commercially prepared soups when too rushed to cook, hot red pepper flakes are a godsend, adding instant flavor and texture, and banishing bland uniformity. They are quite simply medium-hot, dried chili peppers broken into small pieces. In this way the heat is scattered throughout the dish to which they are added rather than disseminated evenly, as it would be if chili powder or cayenne were used. The little red specks of chili pepper also add visual interest.

chili powder
Capsicum frutescens

Chili powder varies somewhat, depending on its country of origin. Indian chili powder, which provides the hot element in curry powder, is very similar to cayenne pepper, and the two can be used interchangeably. They are both made from the dried and ground flesh and seeds of red chilies. In the Southwestern states of the U.S., where chili powder is widely used, it is called chile powder and has other spices and flavorings added, such as cumin, oregano, and garlic.

caraway seeds

Carum carvi

Caraway is a native of northern Europe and Asia, growing wild in the Himalayas and Siberia. It was prized by the Arabs in ancient times, and was believed to have many magical and medicinal properties. It is a member of the same umbelliferous family as fennel and dill, and is very similar to them in appearance. It is a biennial, growing about 2 feet high, with hollow, woody stems and narrow leaves. The seeds are almost identical to those of cumin: small, oval, ribbed, and gray-brown. Caraway is often confused with cumin, especially in France, where it is called *cumin des près*.

Caraway is easy to grow, but there is little point unless you have space to spare, for it takes two years to produce seed. The seed should be sown in autumn, as soon as it has ripened. It needs light, well-drained soil in a sunny spot. The fresh leaves may be treated as an herb and eaten raw, like parsley; the root is also edible.

Caraway seeds are a favorite flavoring in central and northern Europe, especially in Germany, Austria, Finland, and the Scandinavian countries, and are also widely used in Jewish cookery. The German word for caraway is *kümmel*, which is also the name of the liqueur that is made from it. Caraway seeds are used to flavor dishes of sauerkraut, potatoes, pork, and sausages, and they are added to rye bread. In Alsace a dish of roasted caraway seeds is served with the local Müenster cheese. In Great Britain caraway seeds have lost the popularity they enjoyed in Elizabethan times. Then, they were baked in breads and cakes, and made into small sugar-coated sweets called comfits. According to Elizabeth David in her book *English Bread and Yeast Cookery* (Allen Lane, 1977), comfits were often baked in bread rolls and cakes to give a crunchy effect.

Cassia is a native of China, and is now grown widely throughout Southeast Asia. It is one of the ingredients of Chinese Five-Spice Powder (see page 63), and is the Chinese equivalent of cinnamon, to which it is closely related, but is somewhat stronger and coarser in flavor. Like cinnamon, it is sold in two forms: sticks or quills of rolled aromatic bark, and ground into powder. The sticks are thicker and less tightly rolled than those of cinnamon, and are harder. They are difficult to grind at home, so cassia is best bought ground, as needed. Its use should be relegated to savory dishes such as meat, with the more delicate cinnamon reserved for sweet dishes (although in Germany, Italy, and the United States, cassia is used in making chocolate). It also works as a digestive when taken in the form of an infusion.

cassia
Cinnamomum cassia

cinnamon

Cinnamomum zeylanicanum

Cinnamon is the thinly rolled inner bark of an evergreen tree that grows mainly in southern India and Sri Lanka, in Madagascar, and in the West Indies. As well as a flavoring for sweet and savory dishes, cinnamon can be used medicinally; it acts as a digestive and stimulant, and calms the stomach. It is also a natural antiseptic.

Cinnamon is probably most widely used as a flavoring in Turkey and Egypt. It has been known in Great Britain for hundreds of years, but nowadays its use is confined to sweet dishes such as hot cross buns, fruitcakes, and mincemeat, and to mulled wine. A mixture of equal parts of ground cinnamon, nutmeg, and cloves is often used to spice bread and cakes. Yet in medieval times, when spices were in more general use in Great Britain, cinnamon was frequently added to meat or even fish dishes. In the United States cinnamon is widely used in cakes and pastries, often combined with apples, while cinnamon toast is a popular snack. In India cinnamon is commonly used in meat and rice dishes, and in Garam Masala (see page 58). It is also one of the ingredients of commercially manufactured curry powder.

Coriander is believed to have been introduced to the rest of Europe by the Romans, but it is not known whether it was valued for the sake of the berries or the leaves. The berries are more accessible, with their warm "fruity" flavor, and have been popular for hundreds of years. The leaves (usually called cilantro in the U.S.), on the other hand, have only recently regained their popularity, and their availability. Coriander is used extensively, both as a spice and as an herb, in India and Southeast Asia. In Thailand the roots are used more than the leaves or berries.

Coriander is easily grown, as long as the soil is light and friable, and gets plenty of sun. Otherwise the flavor will be poor. The seed should be sown in spring in rows ½ inch deep and 8 inches apart. The berries ripen in late summer, when the plant should be cut and left to dry. Then the heads are collected and the berries harvested. Coriander seeds itself readily if allowed to do so.

A magical spice that seems to enhance other foods, coriander is equally good used alone and in conjunction with other spices. It is delicious mixed in equal parts with cumin, or in complex blends such as Garam Masala and Curry Powder (see pages 58, 60). It is an important part of English pickling spice and dishes cooked *à la grecque*, and is good used with fish, meat, eggs, vegetables, and grains, and in spiced cakes and puddings.

Coriander is immensely popular in Tunisia, where it is combined with garlic, caraway seeds, and dried chilies in a spice blend called Tabil (see page 64). It is also frequently used with ground cinnamon and dried rosebuds.

coriander
Coriandrum sativum

saffron
Crocus sativus

Saffron is made from the dried stigmas of a species of crocus. This bulb grows 6 inches high and has a purple flower in the autumn. It must not be confused with the autumn crocus, *colchicum autumnale*, which also bears purple flowers in the autumn but does not produce leaves until the following spring; the stamens of this crocus are poisonous. Each flower of the *crocus sativus* has only three pistils, and these must first be picked by hand, then the saffron extracted, also by hand. Over 4,000 blooms are required to yield 1 oz. of saffron.

Saffron has always been the most costly of all the spices and, in many countries, the most highly prized. Since the high cost is a result of the labor-intensive nature of its production, it is even more expensive now than in the past, but this is a very potent spice, and ¼–½ teaspoon is the most that any dish should need unless it is being made on a large scale. It has been in use since classical times as a flavoring for food and wine, and as a dye, drug, scent, and cosmetic. It is an effective stimulant and digestive, increasing the flow of saliva and digestive juices. By intensifying the action of the sweat glands, it promotes perspiration. The Romans used it in their baths, and in oil to perfume their bodies.

It seems probable that it was the Romans who brought saffron to Great Britain; it certainly found favor, and was cultivated in Essex, around what became Saffron Walden, for 300–400 years. Although saffron comes from Asia Minor and likes a hot, dry climate, the English saffron was well thought of. The Arabs introduced saffron to Spain,

and the very best is still grown there today, in Valencia. It is also widely cultivated in Kashmir. The saffron crocus grows wild in Iran, but the saffron it produces is a slightly inferior variety, weaker in flavor and color than the Spanish one.

The best known saffron dishes are the Spanish paella, the Italian risotto, and the fish soups of Mediterranean France. In medieval England saffron figured in any number of dishes, sweet and savory alike, but it is only in baked breads and cakes that it is still used today.

Saffron is marketed in two forms: whole threads and ground into a powder. It is usually advisable to buy threads rather than powder, as the latter is easily adulterated, especially in markets in Third World countries, where marigold or safflower stamens, or even turmeric, are often added to, or substituted for, the real thing. As Tom Stobart rightly says in his book *The Cook's Encyclopaedia* (Batsford, 1980), "Cheap saffron does not exist."

A good way to maximize the flavor and color of threads is by first gently toasting them in a metal spoon over low heat, then pounding them in a mortar, adding a couple of spoonfuls of hot liquid — stock, water, or milk — and leaving them to infuse for 5 minutes. The highly colored and aromatic liquid can then be added to a dish, preferably toward the end of its cooking. Powdered saffron can be added instantly to any dish, and is useful in a dry dish when liquid is not desired. But saffron threads can easily be crumbled between the fingers for this purpose too, so do not despair if that is all you have.

cumin
Cuminum cyminum

Cumin shares certain characteristics with coriander: Both originated in the eastern Mediterranean; in both cases it is the fruit, rather than the seed, of the plant that is used as a spice; and both plants are members of the parsley family, *Umbelliferae*. Cumin has narrow, ribbonlike leaves and umbels of small pink or white flowers. The so-called seeds are oblong in shape and grayish in color. Dry roasting cumin before grinding, or using whole seeds, brings out the flavor.

One of the most subtle and delicate of all the Indian "curry" spices, cumin blends remarkably well with coriander and with spice mixtures, as in Garam Masala and Curry Powder (see pages 58, 60). In India both whole and ground cumin are widely used, and black cumin is much esteemed.

Cumin goes well with fish, vegetables, and grains. Its taste is quite pervasive, so use in moderation. It complements cheese superbly, and wild cumin is used in making Müenster cheese in Alsace.

Cumin also has medicinal properties: It helps to dispel flatulence, acts as an antispasmodic, and is effective, when used as a poultice, in relieving aches and pains.

turmeric
Curcuma longa

Turmeric is one of the less distinguished spices, but because of its low price and easy availability it is also one of the more familiar ones. We find it frequently in curry powders, mustards, and relishes such as piccalilli, and as a cheap substitute for saffron. It is often used in marinades, and gives an agreeable yellow coloring, similar to saffron, and an appealing earthy taste to cooked dishes.

The plant is of the same family as ginger, but with broader leaves, and has similar rhizomes, but with bright orange flesh, which turns yellow when dried. In India and Southeast Asia, fresh turmeric is used like fresh ginger, but is much harder to grate or chop. In the West turmeric is available dried, either whole or ground. Because of its rocklike consistency, it is probably best bought ground, but it should be purchased in small quantities and replaced often, for it soon starts to taste musty.

Turmeric is a natural antiseptic and is also used as a dye, perhaps most notably in the yellow robes of Buddhist monks. It grows wild in the tropical countries of southern Asia, and varies in brightness according to where it grows.

lemon grass

Cymbopogon citratus

In its fresh state, lemon grass is usually classified as an herb, but when dried, either whole or in powdered form, it becomes a spice. Called *sereh* in Indonesia and *takrai* in Thailand, lemon grass is an important flavoring in Southeast Asia, where the lemon tree will not grow. It resembles lemon rind more closely than lemon juice, since it lacks the citric acid of the fresh fruit. Lemon peel makes the best substitute for lemon grass; lemon balm and lemon verbena are also good.

The part of lemon grass used in food is the swollen base of the stem, tightly encased in a sheath of leaves, with the roots growing outward from the base. The whole dried stalk should be soaked before being used to flavor a dish, then discarded before the dish is served. The powdered form is easier to use and requires no soaking. One teaspoon of powdered *sereh* equals one stalk fresh lemon grass.

The aromatic essence of cardamom is contained within the seeds: small black objects, crowded together, 10–12 at a time, inside the papery pod. The pistachio-green pods are the best; less good are the larger brown pods or those that have been bleached white. The plant is herbaceous, growing 12 feet high. It is related to ginger, and is widely grown in tropical regions of India, Sri Lanka, and South America.

Cardamom is one of the prime ingredients in Garam Masala and in commercially made Curry Powder (see pages 58 and 60). In Scandinavia and parts of northern Germany and Russia, cardamom is used to flavor liqueurs, while in the Middle East a few cardamom seeds are added to coffee to give that unmistakable perfumed aroma and taste. In the Arab countries the seeds are often chewed, both as a digestive and to sweeten the breath.

cardamom
Elettaria cardamomum

cloves

Eugenia caryophyllus

Cloves are the immature, unopened flower buds of an evergreen tree that grows near the coast of tropical parts of Southeast Asia, east Africa, and the West Indies. It grew first on the Spice Islands, or Moluccas, and was taken to many lands in Europe by the Romans. Cloves were, at that time, as highly regarded as black peppercorns, a true luxury. In the eighteenth century the cultivation of cloves spread to Madagascar and Zanzibar. Today they are grown in southern India, Sri Lanka, Java, Sumatra, Brazil, and the West Indies.

Cloves can be bought whole, still on the stalk, or ground. Unless you plan to use them immediately, it is better to buy them whole, for ground spices soon lose their freshness and taste musty.

Cloves are widely used in conjunction with other spices — usually black peppercorns, nutmeg, and cinnamon — or alone, in savory and sweet dishes, and in drinks. They are commonly stuck in an onion to flavor bread sauce, used to stud the surface of a ham before baking, and stuck in apples before baking. They are also added to mulled wine. In India, cloves are used in meat and rice dishes, and are one of the spices in Garam Masala (see page 58). Use in moderation, for their strong aromatic flavor can become over-assertive.

asafoetida

Ferula asafoetida

Asafoetida is an obscure and fascinating substance, little known in the West today, although it was esteemed by the Romans. It is formed from the sap that flows from the roots of a large umbelliferous plant, very like cow parsley in appearance, which is grown mainly in Iran and India. The roots are cut with a knife in early summer, and the milky sap that seeps out turns into a hard resinlike substance. It is sold either in block form or ground into powder. When bought in blocks, it must be crushed in a mortar before use. In either form it should be stored in an airtight container, for it has a powerful and unpleasant smell. This disappears on contact with heat, and a delicate, oniony flavor develops. For this reason, it is particularly prized by members of Indian sects who are not permitted to eat onions.

As well as flavor, asafoetida has great digestive powers, and helps to combat flatulence. For this reason, it is always used in minute quantities in dishes of dried beans, fresh vegetables, and fish.

fennel seeds

Foeniculum vulgare

Fennel grows wild in southern Europe and in the British Isles. It is very popular in Italy, both as a vegetable and as a flavoring, and the seeds are used in a salami called *finocchiona*, made in Florence. Fennel seeds are also much used in Indian cookery in dishes of meat, fish, and vegetables, and in spice mixtures, and whole roasted seeds are chewed after a meal, as a digestive.

The medicinal properties of fennel are many: an infusion of the seeds can be taken as a stimulant, a digestive, and a sedative, and as a treatment for bronchial troubles, or used as an eyewash.

There are three varieties of fennel. The one to grow for seeds is wild fennel (*Foeniculum vulgare*); the others (*F. officinale* and *F. dulce*) are cultivated for use as a vegetable. Fennel is easily grown, and will self-seed if some of the seeds are left to fall naturally. A perennial, growing about 3–5 feet high, it does well in a sunny spot in well-drained soil. Very like dill, angelica, and caraway in its pattern of growth, although quite distinct in flavor, fennel has hollow woody stems, finely divided leaves, and umbels of yellow flowers. The seeds are very similar to dill but slightly larger, longer, and light greenish-brown. The seed should be sown in spring and may be harvested from midsummer onward. If preferred, the plants may be propagated by root division in the spring, so that all the seeds can be used as a spice. Fennel and dill should not be grown too close together or they will cross-fertilize.

Licorice is a hardy, herbaceous perennial, a member of the pea family. It is native to southwestern Asia, growing wild through Asia Minor. It is a graceful plant, growing 3–4 feet tall, with light, feathery leaves and pale-blue flowers followed by small reddish-brown pods, rather like small pea pods, each containing 3–4 seeds. The tap root grows 3–4 feet deep, and throws off a series of horizontal rhizomes. Both root and rhizomes are used to make the sweet extract for medicinal and other purposes.

Licorice was used by the ancient Greeks as a medicament for curing coughs and other chest ailments. It has been used for the same purposes by the Italians ever since Roman times, and is still much used in this way in Spain, southern France, Germany, Austria, Russia, Greece, and China. It has been cultivated in Great Britain since Elizabethan times, especially in Yorkshire, where its use has been primarily for flavoring confectionery. Until the advent of antibiotics after World War II, it was used to sweeten unpalatable medicines such as cascara. It was also used to darken gingerbread, and to flavor beer, tobacco, and snuff.

Licorice is easily grown in full sun, in a well-drained, rich soil, dug 3–4 feet deep and 6–9 feet wide. It is increased by root division in autumn or spring, and should be permitted to grow undisturbed for 3–5 years before being harvested, in order to allow it time to form a dense root and rhizome system. In their fresh state, the roots and rhizomes are wrinkled and fibrous, brown outside and yellowish within. They can be chewed raw to extract the familiar sweetness, or can be coarsely grated and infused to make a tea, which can be helpful in treating coughs and sore throats. For commercial use, the rhizomes and roots of licorice are ground, boiled, and evaporated to make the root extract, which is then marketed in stick form or ground again as a spice.

licorice
Glycyrrhiza glabra

star anise

Illicium verum

This unmistakable spice is shaped like a star and has a strong smell of aniseed mixed with licorice, like an old-fashioned candy shop. In the center of each petal-shaped pod is an oval seed, light brown and shiny. The tree from which it comes is an evergreen related to the magnolia and grows wild in China and Japan.

Star anise is much used in Chinese cookery, especially in and around Canton. It is also used in some Indonesian countries, and in parts of western India, like Goa, that have traded with China in the past.

The flavor of star anise is similar to ordinary aniseed, but stronger and with a more pronounced licorice element. It is a major ingredient in Chinese Five-Spice Powder (see page 63), and is often added whole to dishes of braised meat and poultry. It may be removed before serving, although in the East whole spices like cinnamon and star anise are often left in the dish and simply pushed to the side of the plate by each diner.

juniper berries
Juniperus communis

There are many wild species of juniper, but the one whose berries are used in food is native to the British Isles and grows throughout most of northern Europe. It is a small tree or shrub, an evergreen conifer with prickly leaves and small yellow flowers. The berries take two to three years to ripen, so that both ripe and unripe berries may be found on the same bush. The green, unripe berries turn purplish-blue as they ripen; later, when dried, they blacken. The ripe berries are picked in the autumn and dried, or semidried, before they are used.

Juniper berries are used primarily in making gin. They are also much used, especially in Central Europe, in marinades, terrines, sauerkraut, and with game, pork, and ham. In Great Britain they figure in traditional recipes for spicing beef. The wood gives off a fragrant smoke when burned, thus scenting a room deliciously.

Juniper berries also have therapeutic uses, as a diuretic and as a treatment for indigestion and flatulence. Juniper is easy to grow, but it is essential to have both male and female plants to achieve a crop of berries.

Galangal is one of those baffling plants that crops up over the centuries in different countries and under different names. In medieval Britain, where it was known as galingale and was highly esteemed, it was probably the root of a plant called *Cyperus longus*. In the Far East, where it is widely used today, it may be one of two plants, greater or lesser galangal, and its Latin name varies from *Kaempferia* to *Alpinia* to *Languas*.

It is worth knowing some of galangal's Eastern names in order to recognize it in Asian markets. Galangal may be found in three forms: fresh, dried whole, and ground. In each of these states it resembles a duller ginger. It is called *laos* and *kencur* in Indonesia; *khaa, kha*, or *ka* in Thailand; and *langhuas* in Malaysia. In its powdered form it is often called *laos* powder.

Whatever its name, it is rarely used today outside Indonesian cuisine. It is not unlike ginger in appearance and flavor: an edible rhizome, duller in color and with a more complex, earthy taste. It has faint overtones of camphor too, with a not unpleasant musky overlay.

galangal
Languas galanga, Cyperus longus

mace
Myristica fragrans

Mace is the dried outer coating of the seed of the nutmeg tree. It grows in broad bands, called blades, forming a net-like cage around the nutmeg. It is sold either whole, in flattened blades, or ground into powder.

Mace is similar to nutmeg in flavor, but with an added earthy overtone. When fresh, the bands of mace are bright red, but they turn a gingery brown when dried. The blades are used whole in dishes that require long cooking, while the powdered form may be added toward the end of cooking. In the West mace is traditionally used in savory dishes, and nutmeg is more often used in sweet dishes. In India, however, both mace and nutmeg are only ever used in savory dishes and in spice mixtures like Garam Masala (see page 58).

The nutmeg tree grew originally in the Molucca Islands, then spread to other parts of Indonesia. The trade in nutmeg and mace was controlled first by Arab traders, then by the Portuguese, then the Dutch, and finally by the English. Mace was very highly esteemed in medieval England, more popular even than nutmeg.

nigella
Nigella sativa

The seed of an otherwise nondescript species of love-in-the-mist, nigella is perhaps better known under its Indian name, *kalonji*, although it is often (wrongly) sold in Indian stores as black onion seed or even as black cumin seed. Once identified, it is not easily forgotten, for this minuscule, heart-shaped seed in dusty jet black, looking rather like coal dust, is unmistakable. It has a weird, earthy flavor, not exactly agreeable when eaten alone, but good in conjunction with other spices or foods. Its crunchy texture is used to good advantage when sprinkled over soft tandoor-baked breads, such as naan, before baking, as is done in northern India. It is also widely used in Bengal in spice mixtures, and in pickling fish and vegetables.

In the countries of the Middle East nigella seeds, called *shamar* in Arabic, are mixed with sesame seeds and sprinkled on bread rolls before baking. They also have therapeutic powers, cleansing the blood of toxins and helping to stimulate the liver. They can be used to treat hepatitis and to improve the complexion.

Nigella sativa is an annual growing 18 inches high, with blue flowers. It is a native of the eastern Mediterranean, North Africa, and the Middle East. Today it grows wild throughout Central Europe and Asia, and is widely cultivated in India and the Middle East.

nutmeg
Myristica fragrans

Nutmeg is the seed of the nutmeg tree. It grows within a lacy cage of mace, inside a fleshy peachlike fruit. It is dried in the sun after harvesting, and is sold both whole and in powdered form. Although very hard to grate, the whole nutmeg may be cracked easily with a hammer. It is best bought whole, as the ground form soon loses its fragrance.

The nutmeg tree grew first in the Molucca Islands, and formed a valuable part of the spice trade. It is now widely grown throughout Indonesia and in Grenada. It is a large tree, growing up to 60 feet high.

Nutmeg has been popular in Great Britain since medieval times, usually for flavoring sweet milky dishes such as custard and rice pudding. It is also paired with vegetables such as onions, cauliflowers, spinach, and potatoes, used in milk-based sauces, in spiced fruitcakes, and in mulled wine.

poppy seeds
Papaver somniferum

The opium poppy, from which the edible seeds are taken, grew first in Asia Minor and has been widely cultivated in Turkey, Iran, India, and China. It is an herbaceous annual growing 1–3 feet tall, with large, pretty, pale flowers. The petals have wavy edges and vary in color from lilac and pink to white and variegated. The seeds are contained in one large seed pod in the center of the flower. If the unripe seed pod is cut open, opium oozes out. The ripe seeds, however, are harmless; they contain merely the poppy seed oil, called *huile d'oeillette* or *olivette* in France, which is used by cooks and artists alike.

Although the seeds do not contain opium, both they and the petals have a slight soporific property, and can be made into a syrup to take as a calming agent for coughs and other bronchial troubles. An infusion of the dried petals can be taken at night as a sedative. Alternatively, according to the great herbalist Maurice Mésségué, a few of the petals may be added to an infusion of lime flowers, or *tilleul*. The flowers may also be made into a poultice for external use in treating inflammation of the eye or eyelid.

There are two types of poppy seed: the more common gray-blue one, and a pale, creamy yellow one, called "white" poppy seed, which comes from a species of poppy that is grown in India and does not produce opium. The gray seed is used in Central European, Balkan, and Slav cooking. In Jewish cuisine it is sprinkled on bagels, bread rolls, cookies, and cakes. In Russia the same seeds are usually boiled, then pounded and mixed with honey for use as a filling for cakes and sweet dishes. In India the white poppy seeds are toasted and then pounded to a paste with a little water and used instead of flour to thicken sauces and curries.

Papaver somniferum is easily grown by sowing in the spring in rich, damp soil in full sun. The seed may be scattered over finely tilled soil or sown in holes 1 foot apart. If left alone, poppies will self-seed with ease, but if growing them just for their seed, they should be harvested as soon as the petals fall. If the petals are to be used, they must be picked at their peak and spread on paper to dry in a sheltered, shady spot in the open air.

allspice
Pimenta dioica

Allspice is the berry of an evergreen tree that grows wild in South America and the West Indies. The berries, which are picked and dried before they ripen, have an interesting flavor. It resembles a mixture of other spices, notably cloves, cinnamon, nutmeg, or mace, hence the name. (It used to be called Jamaica pepper, since this was one of its places of origin.) An easy substitute for allspice can be made by mixing equal parts of ground cinnamon and mace and with ½ part each ground cloves and ground pepper. Or, for savory dishes such as pâtés and terrines, you can use the French mixture *Quatre Epices* (see page 63), which is composed of a similar mixture of spices, but this is too peppery for use in sweet dishes.

In Great Britain allspice has been restricted to sweet dishes, such as puddings and fruit-cakes. In the Middle East, especially in Turkey, it is used predominantly in savory dishes of rice, game, and ground meat. This is a pattern that is repeated over and over.

aniseed

Pimpinella anisum

Aniseed, also called anise, is a member of the hemlock family, and dangerously similar to its poisonous relative. The main difference lies in the seeds, which in the case of aniseed are borne in pairs. Aniseed can be raised only from seed, but it is easily grown in a sunny sheltered spot. It grows about 18 inches high, and has umbels of tiny white flowers in summer. The seeds are grayish-brown, oval, and slightly ridged, and should be gathered in the autumn, unless the plant is to be allowed to self-seed.

Aniseed has a strange, licorice-like flavor, loved by some and abhorred by others. In the Mediterranean countries it is used to flavor aperitifs such as pernod, anisette, ouzo, raki, and arak, while in Central and northern European countries it is used in baking breads and cakes. In Southeast Asia and in India it is used in curries, most predominantly with fish.

Aniseed has powerful medicinal properties, mainly as a digestive, a stimulant for a sluggish system, and a cure for flatulence. It has been used to these ends in China and India since ancient times. Its digestive powers explain why it is used in so many Mediterranean aperitifs, while in India the seeds are often chewed after a meal, both as a digestive and to sweeten the breath. An effective treatment for indigestion can be made by pouring 4⅜ cups boiling water onto 1 teaspoon aniseed, leaving it for approximately 4–5 minutes, then drinking the aniseed and water mixture three times a day until the condition is alleviated.

cubebs

Piper cubeba

A form of pepper now rarely seen outside the East Indies and North Africa, cubebs are the fruit of a perennial vine related to the true pepper vine, *Piper nigrum*. The cubeb vine grows wild in Java and Sumatra. It is often cultivated on coffee plantations, growing in the shade of the coffee bushes. The unripe berries, slightly larger than peppercorns, are dried before use. They are sometimes called "tailed pepper," as each berry has a stem attached. They have a slightly bitter flavor, halfway between pepper and allspice, and were once used like pepper by the Arabs, who introduced them to Europe. Cubebs were popular in medieval Britain as a flavoring for food and as a medicament, but their use diminished and has never been revived.

Medicinally, cubebs have much the same properties as pepper, and may be used ground or as an infusion. They are effective when used as a stimulant or to expel gas from the stomach, and can be used to treat cystitis and bronchitis.

pepper

Piper nigrum

Pepper has a fascinating history, as it was one of the first spices to reach the West from the East, and has been one of, if not *the*, most highly valued spices ever since. References to pepper have been found in Greek and Roman writings dating back to the fifth century BC, and it was considered literally worth its weight in gold by the Romans.

Black, white, and green peppercorns are the berries of the climbing vine *Piper nigrum*, which grows wild in the tropical forests of Asia. The very best come from the Malabar coast in southern India. The berries are green before they ripen, when they turn bright red. Black peppercorns are the unripe berries that have been picked by hand and left to dry in the sun for several days, whereupon they shrivel up, harden, and turn dark brown. White peppercorns have been allowed to ripen on the vine, and then are picked, also by hand, soaked, and milled to remove the outer skin. White peppercorns lack the aromatic quality of the black; their only virtue seems to be for fussy cooks who object to the look of black specks in pale dishes.

Green peppercorns are also picked before they ripen, and then are freeze-dried, pickled, or simply preserved in cans or jars. They can sometimes be bought fresh, still on the stem. In whatever state you buy them, green peppercorns are still soft enough to be squashed between the fingers, and have a mild, fresh, sappy taste.

Both black and white pepper are best used freshly ground, for they soon lose their aromatic qualities. As Jill Norman points out in her excellent book, *The Complete Guide to Spices* (Dorling Kindersley, 1990), "Pepper is neither sweet nor savory, just pungent, and can therefore be used in both types of dish." (See Strawberries with Black Pepper, page 239.)

Pepper also has its uses in promoting health. Taken ground, as a powder, it acts as a stimulant and is effective in expelling gas from the stomach and in reducing fever. It is also effective as a digestive, to treat flatulence, and as a diuretic. Pepper has one disadvantage: it can cause congestion of the blood vessels, and therefore its use should be avoided, or minimized, by people suffering from varicose veins or hemorrhoids.

Pink peppercorns are the berries of an unrelated South American plant, *schinus molle*. Nonetheless, they have a definite taste of pepper, although milder and sweeter than the real thing. Their advantage, which has made them popular, is their visual appeal. They are often sold mixed with green and black peppercorns, and are used mainly as a color contrast.

Pistacia lentiscus

mastic

This is a strange substance not much seen outside the Middle East and the Balkans. Formed naturally from the resinous sap of the low-growing, bushy, evergreen lentisk tree, it looks for all the world like candy: irregular lumps of pale amber-colored crystal. It is often chewed with a piece of wax, like chewing gum, when it gives off an aromatic taste, like chewing pine needles. The gum has a strange, smoky flavor. Its main use lies in flavoring sweet dishes such as the Greek Rice Pudding (see page 234) and Turkish delight. It must be pounded or crushed before use, usually in conjunction with sugar and rosewater. The lentisk tree, a species of pine tree, grows wild in Greece, Turkey, and the Middle East, especially on the Greek island of Chios, which exports mastic in large quantities.

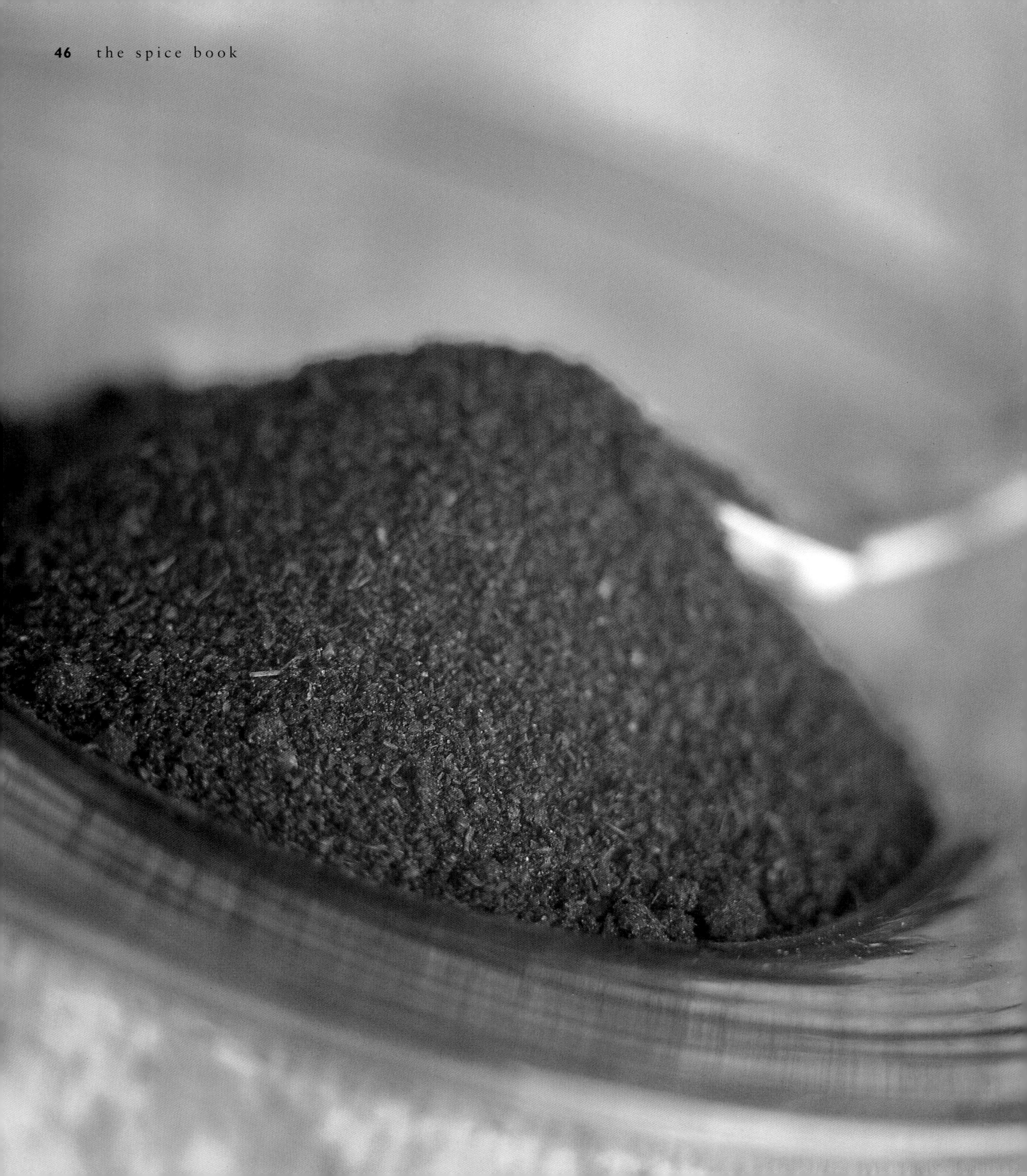

Rosa damascena
coeurs des roses

The dried buds of a species of Damask rose, called *rous el word* in Arabic, *coeurs des roses* are much used as a flavoring agent in the countries of the Maghreb. Usually included in the multitude of spices that are combined to make Ras el Hanout (see page 65), *coeurs des roses* also figure in the Tunisian spice mixture called *Quatre Epices* (see page 63), not to be confused with the French mixture of the same name.

Sold loose in sacks in the spice markets, these pretty pinkish-red blossoms have a delicate fragrance, and are very aromatic. They are used for savory and sweet dishes alike, usually in conjunction with other sweet-flavored spices, such as cinnamon.

Sumac is made from the dried berries of a large shrub that grows in temperate regions throughout the Middle East and around the Mediterranean. It grows 3–10 feet high, and has greenish-white flowers borne in panicles in July and August. These are followed by small red berries that ripen slowly. Just before the berries are ripe, the boughs are cut and the berries are left to dry on the branch in the sun. The dried berries are later ground into a coarse red powder, the color of dried blood, which has a pleasantly sour taste, like salt and lemon juice combined. The powder is used as a spice in Iran, Iraq, Turkey, and most of the Middle Eastern countries, especially Lebanon.

The spice is used mainly in salad dressings and in marinades for fish, chicken, and meat. In other words, it is used in much the same way as lemon juice. It is also one of the three ingredients, with wild thyme and sesame seeds, of the Middle Eastern spice mixture called Za'atar (see page 62).

The sap of the bush is poisonous, and the branches should be handled with care, for some people are allergic even to their touch. A substance obtained from the leaves is used to tan and dye leather.

sumac
Rhus coriaria

sesame seeds

Sesamum indicum

Sesame is an annual, growing 2–3 feet high, with pale pink or white flowers. It grows wild in Morocco and India; in colder climates it is best grown under glass, in a heated greenhouse or conservatory. The seed that forms after the flowers have faded comes in three colors: pearly white, cream, and black. The last is rarely seen in the West, except in Asian markets, but is very popular in Japan. Of all the seeds, I find sesame the most delicious, almost addictive. They are also one of the most nutritious, being rich in vitamins and minerals — and very high in calories.

Sesame seeds are ground into two oils, both useful in different ways. One is a light, refined oil, almost flavorless, good for frying and dressing light salads. The other is a rich, complex oil, dense in flavor, made with the toasted seeds. This is very concentrated, and only a few drops are needed. It is much used as a flavoring in China and Japan.

In the Middle East sesame seeds are ground into tahini, an oily paste rather like a smooth peanut butter. Nutritious and fattening, tahini is used as the basis of many delicious, oily spreads such as hummus, made with garbanzos, and *baba ghanouj*, made with roasted eggplants.

Like most seeds, sesame seeds are greatly enhanced by a preliminary roasting in a skillet pan over gentle heat for 2–3 minutes. They can then be scattered over salads, cooked vegetables or — almost best of all — thick slices of brown bread and butter. They form part of the excellent spice mixture called Dukkah (see page 62), which may be eaten in the same way.

mustard seeds

Sinapsis alba, Brassica juncea, B. nigra

There are three basic mustard seeds: white (*Sinapsis alba*), which is also called yellow; brown (*Brassica juncea*), which is also called oriental; and black (*B. nigra*). Brown mustard comes in two forms, one with a light brown coat, and the other with a black coat. True black mustard is rarely seen anymore, since it is an noncommercial crop and has been replaced by brown mustard. Both black and white mustard grew first in southern Europe, while brown mustard is a native of India. All three are easily grown in the garden, although black mustard is an unruly crop. The leaves of white mustard may be eaten at the seedling stage, as in mustard and cress, while many varieties of brown mustard are good eaten raw in salads or cooked in stir-fries.

English mustard is made with a combination of brown, with a light brown coat, and white mustard seeds. The combination of the two seeds is vital; the white mustard gives heat on the tongue, the brown mustard gives a volatile heat at the back of the throat, like curry powder, making the eyes water. English is the hottest of all the mustards. The strength varies slightly from year to year, depending on the weather and the country of origin. English mustard also differs from other mustards in that it is usually sold dry, to be mixed to a paste with cold water, thus keeping its fiery strength indefinitely. (Prepared mustards lose some heat each time they are exposed to the air.)

French mustard is made mainly in and around Dijon, Bordeaux, and Meaux, not far from Paris. The best known of these outside France is Dijon mustard, which is made from brown mustard seeds only, mixed with white wine and spices. This is milder than English mustard. A whole grain mustard often called *à l'ancienne* has recently been revived and is very popular. One of the best known is made at Meaux.

German mustard is made with white mustard seeds only, with sugar and herbs added. It is quite mild and slightly sweet. American mustard is very mild, and even sweeter; this is also made with white mustard seeds alone, but colored bright yellow with turmeric. Not generally appreciated by gourmets, it is good with the ubiquitous hot dog.

Mustard's force is invalidated by heat, which destroys the enzymes. For this reason, dry mustard must always be mixed with cold water. For the same reason, mustard can be added in fairly generous quantities to a cooked sauce or casserole without overheating it, yet retaining the flavor. The enzyme activity is also hindered by mixing with acids, such as vinegar, lemon juice, and wine; another reason why English mustard is so much hotter than French and German ones may be that it is only ever mixed with water.

Mustard seeds also have their uses in cooking. In India, whole brown mustard seeds are heated in oil at the start of the cooking, usually in fish or vegetable dishes, while ground mustard seeds are also used, together with other ground seeds, such as poppy and fenugreek, as a thickening agent. Whole white mustard seeds are a natural preservative, used in pickling. Prepared mustard is much used in French cookery as a flavoring for sauces and casseroles, such as *lapin à la moutarde* and *sauce Robert*.

The tamarind is a graceful tree which grows to about 40–60 feet tall, the only species of its genus. Its origins are unknown, but it has been cultivated in India for centuries. It was known in Great Britain in medieval times, and was taken to the West Indies by the Spaniards in the sixteenth and seventeenth centuries. It is now cultivated widely in India, and in the East and West Indies.

The tree is an evergreen, with light green leaves and yellow flowers striped with red. These are followed by light brown, hairy pods 3–6 inches long and 1 inch wide, looking like fat fava bean pods. Each pod contains 4–10 seeds, which are surrounded by a sticky dark red paste threaded through with fibrous strings.

Tamarind can be bought in three forms: fresh, still in the pods; in rectangular blocks of sticky pulp, seeds and fibers, semidried and compressed; and as a concentrate, a thick, dark-red purée. To make tamarind water, simply break off the brittle shells, pull away the fibrous threads, and pour boiling water over the contents of the pods. Leave to cool, then, using the fingers, pull away the pulp and discard the seeds. Push the pulp through a small food mill or coarse sieve, using a little of the soaking water to help it through.

To use the compressed form, break off as much as you need and put it in a bowl. Pour over enough hot water to cover it, then leave it for about 1 hour. Then, working with the fingers, loosen the pulp by pulling and squeezing, and push it through a coarse sieve, using a little of the soaking water to moisten it.

To use the concentrate, dilute as much as you need with a little hot water. The concentrate is certainly the quickest and simplest form to use, but it is not always available in the stores.

In India tamarind is also prized for its medicinal properties. It is used to treat upsets of the stomach and bowels, and as a laxative, an astringent, for fever relief, and as a natural antiseptic. The leaves are used, boiled down to an essence, to treat jaundice and dysentery.

tamarind

Tamarindus indica

Fenugreek is an ancient herb, which was much used medicinally by the Greeks and Egyptians. It was also used as cattle fodder by the Greeks, hence its name, which means "Greek hay." (It is still used as fodder today.) It grew first around the Mediterranean, and was later grown widely in India, as it still is.

Fenugreek is an annual, a member of the pea and clover family, which bears its seeds in tiny pods. It has small, pale-yellow flowers, while the seeds are small, dusty-yellow, and almost square. They are rockhard and must be ground in a mortar before use; an electric spice mill or coffee grinder is not strong enough. Fenugreek is usually roasted before grinding, otherwise the seeds are almost tasteless, but the roasting must be gentle or the seeds will become bitter. They may also be sprouted, like mung beans, and eaten raw in salads; treated in this way they are extra nutritious, for during the process of germination the vitamin B and C content increases considerably, as does the enzyme content. Sprouted fenugreek is also a valuable source of protein, and was useful in the past for its effective anti-scurvy properties; it provided an easily accessible source of fresh food on board ship.

Much used in Indian cookery, fenugreek is a basic ingredient of Curry Powder (see page 60), although it does not figure in garam masala, possibly because it needs long cooking to bring out its flavor, and garam masala is often added only at the end of the cooking time. Fenugreek is used in dishes of fish, meat and vegetables in Indian cuisine, and in bread in North Africa.

The leaves are also used, both fresh and dried, in Indian cookery; they have a slightly bitter taste. They are sometimes found, called *methi*, in Indian markets. Fenugreek is easily grown from seed, so long as the seed is relatively fresh.

Medicinally, fenugreek has many functions. It acts as a digestive and as a stimulant, and is thought to encourage the appetite. For this reason it was popular with Egyptian men, who encouraged their womenfolk to eat lots of it, as they liked them to be fat.

fenugreek
Trigonella foenum-graecum

vanilla
Vanilla planifolia

The vanilla pod is the fruit of a climbing orchid that grows wild in the forests of Central America. Even before the arrival of the Spanish conquistadors at the end of the fifteenth century, it was used by the Aztecs to flavor chocolate. It was taken back to Spain, along with chocolate, by the Spaniards, and the two substances continued to be used together.

In the wild, vanilla grows 30–45 feet high, sprawling over trees and anything else that will act as a support. When cultivated, it is grown over trellises or small trees to facilitate the harvesting of the pods. Each pod grows 8–12 inches long, and contains a number of tiny black seeds, packed with flavor. The pods are picked when they are yellow, before they ripen. During the lengthy curing process they turn black, and their unique flavor develops as the result of enzyme activity. After curing, the pods are jet black with tiny white crystals frosting their outer surface.

The best vanilla comes from Madagascar, where it is widely cultivated, as it is in the East and West Indies. Genuine vanilla is expensive, due in part to its lengthy curing process; and nowadays it is often replaced by a synthetic flavoring called vanillin. Although the purest flavor is obtained by using the pod itself, or sugar flavored by the pods, both vanilla extract and vanilla essence can be quite good when made with the real pods soaked in alcohol. It is important to look for the word "pure" on the label before making your purchase; otherwise you may find you have bought a synthetic flavoring. You can make your own vanilla essence by soaking a split vanilla pod in a small bottle of pure alcohol, such as vodka, for 2–3 weeks before using.

Even the true extracts and essences must be used with care, for it is easy to overdo it, and vanilla, like saffron, is good only when used in judicious quantities. The great advantage of the pod itself is that it gives a subtle flavor that is never overpowering.

Vanilla sugar is a good and inexpensive way of flavoring; this is best made at home, for the commercially made kind is often flavored with the dread vanillin. Simply split a vanilla pod and scrape the seeds into a jar of granulated sugar, adding the split pod as well. From time to time through the coming months add another vanilla pod, either a newly bought one — they are often sold in pairs, when only one is needed — or one that you have used to infuse in milk, then rinsed and dried. By now, I have 40 vanilla pods, some dating back three or four years, stuck in a huge glass jar of sugar, which I replenish from time to time.

Since the orchid is a tropical plant, and such a vigorous one, vanilla is not suitable for growing at home, for it would need a large, heated greenhouse or conservatory to accommodate it. It also needs to be pollinated artificially when cultivated. Buy the true vanilla pod as and when you need it, and enjoy its very special aromatic character.

wasabi

Wasabia japonica

Although known in the West as Japanese horseradish, wasabi is unrelated to true horseradish (*Armoracia rusticana*). Wasabi is a perennial plant, which grows, rather like watercress, on the marshy edges of rivers and streams. The rhizomes are eaten very finely grated: they are light green, with a delicious, hot, sharp, fresh taste, like a cross between horseradish and English mustard. In Japan, special graters, finer than any European or American grater, are made for grating wasabi and ginger. They are produced in three or four sizes, in copper coated with tin, and shaped like small, flat spades, with tiny triangular spikes facing two ways, which reduce the root to a fine, juicy pulp.

Wasabi is always served with sushi and sashimi, two superlative Japanese raw fish dishes, piled on the side of the plate in a little cone like a miniature Mount Fuji. Together with a dipping sauce made with soy sauce and mirin, this sets off the bland flavor of the raw fish to perfection. (A little of the grated wasabi is sometimes stirred into the dipping sauce by each diner.)

The root itself cannot be bought in the West, but wasabi can be found in Japanese markets in two forms: powdered, in small cans; and as a paste, in tubes. The powdered wasabi must be mixed, like mustard, with a little warm water; the prepared paste is used as it comes from the tube.

It is not practical to think in terms of growing wasabi, since the difficulty of finding a source of clean running water is almost as great as that of finding the root to plant outside Japan.

Zanthoxylum piperitum, Fagara piperitum
Szechuan pepper

Also called anise pepper and fagara, Szechuan pepper is made from the seed casings of a species of prickly ash that grows wild in China. The reddish brown berries are picked in the autumn and left to dry in the sun; when the casings burst open, the small black seeds inside are discarded, for they have a bitter taste. The chestnut-brown seed casings are then gently roasted and ground for use as a food flavoring much used in the province of Szechuan.

This species of prickly ash is a semihardy deciduous shrub or bushy tree, growing about 10 feet high, with sharp prickles and small white flowers borne in panicles. Szechuan pepper is one of the ingredients of Chinese Five-Spice Powder (see page 63). It is not exactly hot, but has a curious, slightly numbing effect on the tongue.

Both bark and berries have been used medicinally for centuries. The bark is crushed or powdered and used as a compress for healing wounds, toothaches, and headaches. The berries are used in the form of an infusion; they are antispasmodic as well as gas-reducing, good for treating dyspepsia and indigestion. They also cause perspiration, thus reducing fevers, as well as acting as a stimulant in helping the circulation of the blood and banishing lethargy. (For more information, see also Sansho, page 55.)

sansho

Zanthoxylum piperitum,
Fagara piperitum

This is the Japanese form of Szechuan pepper (see page 54), sometimes called Japanese pepper. It is made from the dried seed casings of the same prickly ash tree as the Chinese variety. In Japan, sansho is considered to be an aid to the digestion of rich and fatty foods, and is always served as accompaniment to grilled eel. In small, old-fashioned restaurants in Tokyo that specialize in this delicacy, sansho is served in a shaker, together with the strips of grilled eel lying on a bed of rice in a rectangular red lacquer box, with a tiny dish of pickles and some thin strips of *nori* (dried seaweed). Sansho has a most unusual taste, rather like a cross between lemon grass and black pepper. It has the same strange, slightly numbing effect on the tongue as Szechuan pepper. The Japanese also serve it with chicken and duck.

In spring the young leaves, called *kimone*, of the prickly ash are picked and used as a garnish for many Japanese dishes, and to flavor vinegar.

Zingiber officinale
ginger

Ginger is an ancient plant, used in China both as a flavoring for food and as a medicament since the sixth century BC. It grows wild in Southeast Asia, China, and Japan. Today India, west Africa, and the West Indies are the largest growers of ginger for export. It is a perennial, whose leafy stems grow roughly 3 feet tall, from rhizomes lying just below the surface of the soil. These rhizomes are the edible part, and are used fresh, dried, pickled as well as preserved in syrup.

Ginger may be grown from a 2 inch piece of rhizome, as long as it has a couple of buds. It should be planted 2 inches deep in rich compost, either in a greenhouse or indoors as a house plant. However, it will produce the large, fleshy rhizomes used for culinary purposes only when grown in a tropical climate.

Ginger is aromatic, therapeutic, and immensely effective used either as a medicament or as a flavoring. Its medicinal powers are numerous. In the East it is used in baths for toning up the system and for relieving muscular aches and pains, and it is taken internally as a digestive and to warm up the whole organism. In Tudor England it was held to be an aphrodisiac.

Fresh ginger is usually classified as a food flavoring, being neither an herb nor a spice, so for the purposes of this book we are dealing with ginger in its dried, ground form: the golden brown, aromatic powder that has been a favorite spice in northern Europe since Roman times. In medieval France and England, spiced gingerbread was gilded with gold leaf and tooled like leather. In Thomas Hardy's England, spiced gingerbread and ginger biscuits (cookies) were traditional "fairings," bought by young men at country fairs to give to their girlfriends. In *Good Things in England* by Florence White (Jonathan Cape, 1932), a collection of English "folk" recipes from 1399 to 1932, Miss White lists no fewer than 15 recipes for ginger biscuits, cakes, and parkins, varying from county to county.

Ginger wine, an excellent cold-weather drink, has been manufactured in Great Britain since the first half of the eighteenth century and is still available today. Drunk with whiskey, it has long been a favorite of mine, a last resort in time of chill, exhaustion, or depression. Ginger beer is another old-fashioned drink that is still popular in Great Britain.

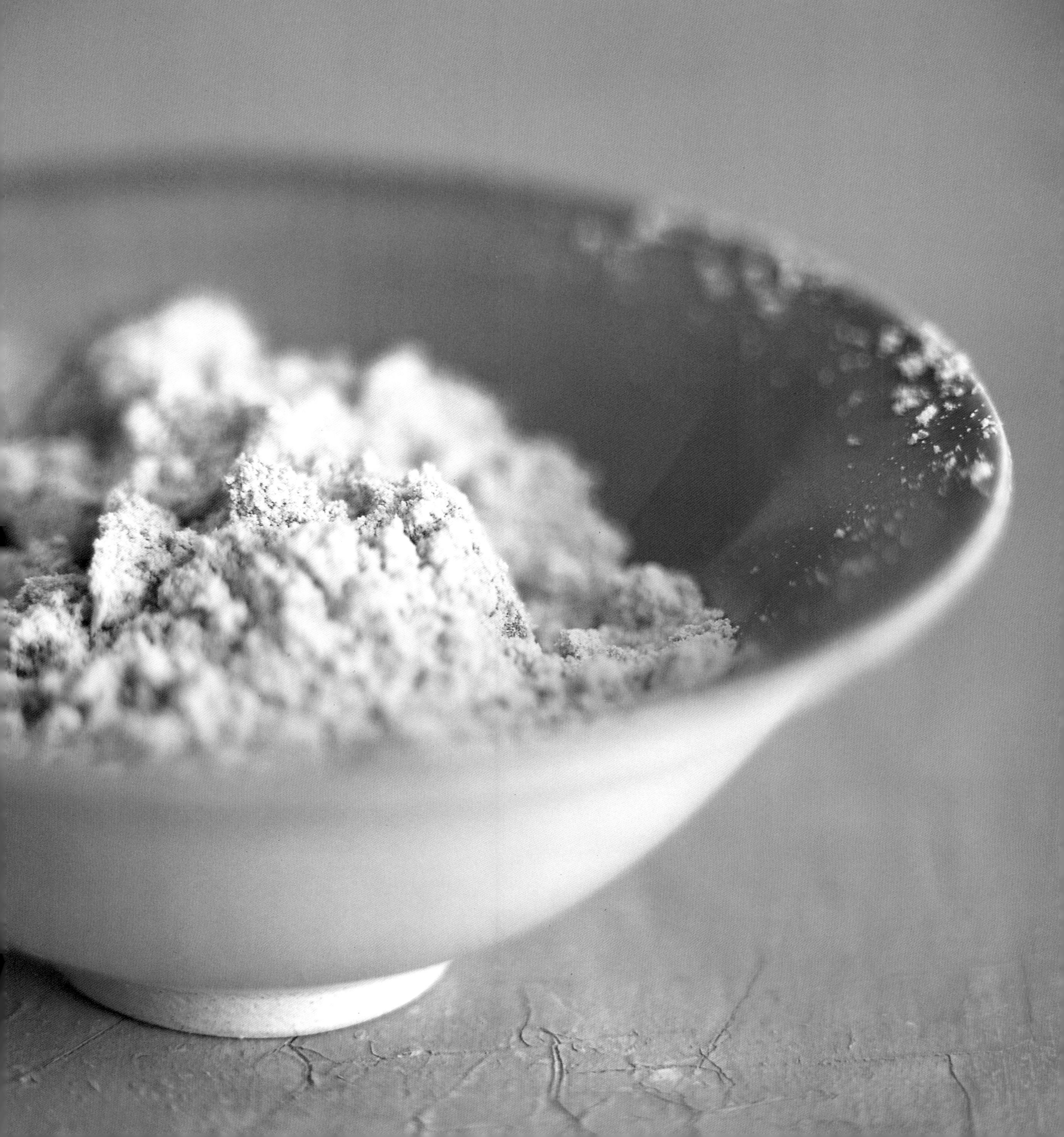

spice mixtures

garam masala

1 oz. coriander seeds

1 oz. cumin seeds (preferably black)

1 3-inch long cinnamon stick, broken into small pieces

1 teaspoon whole cloves

1 teaspoon black peppercorns

12 green cardamom pods, shelled

½ teaspoon ground mace or nutmeg

2 bay leaves, finely crumbled

This mixture is a northern Indian speciality, and varies from region to region, and from household to household. It is less complex than curry powder, being composed for the most part of five or six spices in varying proportions. It is almost always added to dishes at the end of cooking, or even just before serving, as we might add salt and pepper.

According to Julie Sahni, whose book Classic Indian Cooking (Dorling Kindersley, 1986) is one of the best, garam masala has changed its character in recent years. What was originally a sharp, pungent seasoning has become milder and sweeter, due in part to the inclusion of cumin and coriander, which were not part of the original masala. Nowadays the mix usually consists of cardamom, cinnamon, cloves, cumin, coriander, and black peppercorns. Nutmeg and/or mace and bay leaves are sometimes included.

Mix the coriander, cumin, cinnamon, cloves, peppercorns, and shelled cardamoms. Grind them together in a small mill or pound in a mortar (this is hard work). Mix the ground spices with the mace or nutmeg and finely crumbled bay leaves. Pour through a funnel into a small glass jar and seal tightly. Store in a cool, dark cupboard, where it will keep for about 2 months.

Makes 3 oz.

harissa

Harissa comes from Tunisia, where it is invariably served with the bland but delicious couscous. It is also found in Morocco, Libya, and Algeria. It is very hot indeed, and rivals the Indonesian sambal oelek *in strength. Its main ingredient is puréed dried red chilies, with additions of coriander, caraway, and garlic.*

It is hardly worth the effort of making harissa at home, as it is a troublesome business, involving large quantities of hot red chilies, seeds and all. It can now be bought quite easily in small cans and tubes in stores selling North African goods. Harissa can also be found in French markets, since the French became addicted to couscous during their years in the Maghreb, and still eat it often back in France. Alternatively, use sambal oelek, *which can be bought in Indonesian shops and Asian supermarkets, or Hot Sauce II (see page 185) as a substitute. However, if you really do wish to make your own, here is a basic recipe.*

2 oz. dried chili peppers, split and deseeded
2 tablespoons chopped garlic
1 tablespoon sea salt
1 oz. caraway seeds
1–1½ tablespoons olive oil

Soak the dried chilies in tepid water for 3–4 minutes, then chop them very finely and pound in a mortar. Add the garlic and sea salt and continue to pound until reduced to a pulp. Add caraway seeds and pound again. When all is smoothly blended, pack into a tiny jar and cover the surface with the olive oil. Seal tightly.

Makes 5 oz.

curry powder

Curry powder is not an Indian concept. It is the European solution to the annoying question of how to make a curry in the simplest possible way, without having to resort to a pestle and mortar. But this is no longer necessary, with technical aids such as blenders, food processors, and — best of all in this context — small electric spice mills or coffee grinders. (However, the really hard spices, such as fenugreek, still need a mortar.) Now we can make up our own spice mixtures in a matter of seconds, so there is no excuse for the out-of-date cans of curry powder so many of us used to keep in our cupboards.

In the Indian kitchen a fresh masala, or spice mixture, is ground for each dish, using the relevant spices. That is perhaps going too far for most of us in the West, unless we are enthusiasts of such things, but we can at least make up our own blend of curry powder — or even two or three — at frequent intervals, and use it as desired. Often we want just a hint of curry spices; in a sauce, for instance, or an egg croquette, or a fish cake, and in this context a freshly made curry powder does have its uses.

In her book Curries and Bugles (Viking, 1990), Jennifer Brennan suggests that curry powder as we know it was probably dreamed up by an Indian Army officer who had become addicted to curries and wanted a ready-made mix to take home to give his cook.

Many Englishmen became addicted to curry. According to The Raj at Table (Faber & Faber, 1993), David Burton's excellent book, George V was a lover of curry and ate it almost daily, while his mother, Queen Victoria, employed two Indian chefs to prepare curries for the luncheon table every day.

1 oz. coriander seeds
½ oz. cumin seeds (preferably black)
¼ oz. black mustard seeds
¼ oz. black peppercorns
½ oz. fenugreek, whole seeds or ground
6 cardamom pods
4 tablespoons ground turmeric
2 tablespoons chili powder
1 tablespoon ground ginger

Toast all the whole seeds and the cardamom pods in a heavy skillet over gentle heat for 4 minutes, shaking them occasionally. Then leave them to cool. Shell the cardamom pods and grind all the seeds together in a mortar. (If you do not possess a mortar, buy the fenugreek already ground, and grind the other spices in an electric mill or coffee grinder.) Mix all the spices, ground and milled, in a bowl, then pour them into a jar and close tightly. Store the jar in a dark cupboard.

Note: Optional additions are cloves, cinnamon, and curry leaves.

Makes 4½ oz.

dried chilies
and other flavorings

In a spell of hot, dry weather, ripe (red) chilies may be dried simply by leaving them laid out, without touching each other, in a warm room. In their native lands they are dried on racks in the sun, but in a cooler, damper climate they are best dried in the oven.

Lay the chilies on a cookie sheet so that they do not touch each other; then place the sheet in a very cool preheated oven — 225°F — allowing 1½ hours for tiny chilies, and 2½ hours for the larger ones measuring about 2½ inches long. When the time is up, turn off the oven and leave the chilies in the oven to cool. Later, when they have cooled completely, pack them into jars or plastic bags, or thread them on pieces of string. They will keep their flavor almost indefinitely.

Although it cannot be classified as a spice, the peel of citrus fruit can be dried in the same way. This is a very useful flavoring, and an economical one, since it leaves the rest of the fruit intact for eating, for cooking, or for juice. A strip of dried orange peel is added to fish soups in Mediterranean France, and to slow-cooked daubes of beef in Provence. The bitter Seville orange is also good used in this way, and since its season is so short, it is only sensible to prolong it by drying. The Japanese use dried peel of the mandarin (citrus reticulata), which is widely cultivated in Japan. Related to the tangerine, it is very juicy and has its own very special, sharp flavor. It is used in the spice blend called Shichimi Togarishi (see page 64). Two or three different citrus peels, dried and stored in glass jars, make a decorative and useful addition to your kitchen shelves. Lay broad, thin strips of peel, avoiding the white pith, on a cookie sheet and put it in a warm place, such as the top oven when the bottom oven is on, or a plate warmer or airing cupboard — even a cool oven is too hot. Leave them for most of a day, or as long as is convenient.

While the oven is on, drying out the chilies, why not dry a few other foods as well? Dried tomatoes are quite delicious, and easy to do. Small cherry tomatoes and the solid plum tomatoes are both good for this purpose. Cut the cherry tomatoes across in half, and the plum tomatoes in slices ½ inch thick, and lay them on cookie sheets. Both kinds will take about 2 hours to dry, then another hour in the cooling oven. Do not try to keep them, as they will probably become moldy. But they are so delicious served as a small snack, with drinks, that they will probably be eaten up immediately.

Wild mushrooms, or any large mushrooms, can be cut in ½ inch slices and laid on cookie sheets. (Slice caps and stems separately.) Allow 1½ hours in the oven, then another hour in the cooling oven. Cool completely before packing into jars or threading on string. These can be kept for 2–3 months, but if you plan to keep them this long, it is better to store them in jars.

za'atar

The word Za'atar means wild thyme in Arabic, but in this context it means a blend of wild thyme with sesame seeds and sumac, a spice ground from the berries of a Middle Eastern tree. It is very popular in the Lebanon, where the village bakers spread it on flat, round loaves before baking, and sell them straight out of the oven.

Put all the ingredients in a mortar or small electric mill or coffee grinder. Grind thoroughly, then pour into a small container and close tightly. Keep in a dark, cool place — the refrigerator is ideal — and use within 6–8 weeks. Before use, mix with about half its volume of olive oil, until you have a coarse grainy paste.

4 tablespoons sesame seeds, toasted
3 tablespoons dried thyme
2 tablespoons sumac

dukkah

This is an Egyptian spice mixture, also found in other Middle Eastern countries, including Syria and Lebanon. One of my favorite "fast foods," it is easily made at home. The recipe varies slightly from place to place, and from family to family. The base is made of roasted sesame seeds. To this are added either hazelnuts or roasted garbanzos — I often use a mixture of the two — roasted coriander and cumin seeds, salt, and black peppercorns. Wild mountain thyme is sometimes included.

Although it may be made in a processor, care must be taken not to overdo it. As Claudia Roden, an authority on Egyptian food, insists, the mixture should be coarsely ground and dry, not overprocessed to an oily paste.

This is a spice mixture designed to be eaten dry rather than used in cooking. Dukkah is usually eaten with flat (pita) bread and a dish of olive oil. The bread is dipped first in oil, then in the dry spice mixture. I love to eat it with warm, freshly hard-boiled eggs and thick slices of whole grain bread and butter.

¾ **cup sesame seeds**
2 oz. whole cumin seeds
¾ **cup roasted garbanzos or skinned hazelnuts**
8 tablespoons ground coriander
2 teaspoons sea salt
½ **teaspoon black peppercorns**

Toast the sesame seeds in a dry skillet over gentle heat for about 3 minutes, turning them from time to time with a spatula. As they color lightly and start to jump around, remove them from the heat and pour them into a food processor. Toast the cumin seeds in the same way; then add them to the sesame seeds in the processor, with the garbanzos or skinned hazelnuts, coriander, salt, and black peppercorns. Process until finely blended, then turn the mixture into a mortar and pound until even more finely ground. (This final stage is not essential and can be omitted.) Pour or spoon into jars with tightly fitting lids, and store in the refrigerator or a cool, dark cupboard or pantry. Dukkah can be kept for some weeks, but it is at its best soon after making.

Makes about 13 oz.

quatre épices

This is a well-known spice mixture in France, much used in the seasoning of pâtés and terrines. It is easily made at home, since the ingredients are readily available. The usual "four spices" are nutmeg, cinnamon, cloves, and white pepper. Sometimes ginger replaces the cinnamon. The proportions are roughly 4 parts of white peppercorns, 2 parts nutmeg, 1 part each cinnamon (or ginger), and cloves. Without the pepper, it closely resembles the old English mixed spice or pudding spice, or allspice.

In Tunisia the term quatre épices means something far more exotic. This is white pepper and cinnamon combined with paprika and coeurs des roses, a delicious mixture that can be used equally well in sweet and savory dishes.

gomasio

This is a simple and delicious seasoning of toasted sesame seeds and sea salt. It originated in Japan, where sesame seeds are a favorite condiment, to add a nutty taste and crunchy texture to food. It has been taken up in recent years by vegetarians and health food devotees in the United States, where it is called "gomashio," and in Great Britain, where it is sometimes called "sesame salt."

I make it frequently as a simple alternative to Dukkah (see page 62), and eat it in the same way: for snack meals, with hard-boiled eggs, brown bread and butter, and on salads of raw or cooked vegetables. Use it instead of, not as well as, salt.

It can be bought in health food stores, but is quickly made at home. Simply toast 5–6 tablespoons sesame seeds gently in a dry skillet until they change color slightly and start to jump around. Leave them to cool, then mix with 1 tablespoon sea salt and grind in a small mill. Do not overprocess them; the texture should be coarse and fairly uneven. Gomasio keeps well in a tightly closed jar in the refrigerator, but is at its best when freshly made.

Chinese five-spice powder

This familiar Chinese seasoning has a pronounced licorice flavor, which arouses strong feelings for or against it. This is due to the star anise, which is a potent flavoring. The other spices are Szechuan pepper, fennel, cloves, and cinnamon or cassia.

It is available ready-made in Chinese and other Asian stores and supermarkets, packaged in plastic bags or small jars. It is best bought in small quantities and used sparingly in marinades and slow-cooked dishes of pork, poultry, or other meats. It can also be mixed with sea salt and served as a dip, like Dukkah (see page 62), with crudités or hard-boiled eggs.

Five spice powder can also be made at home, although some of the spices are hard to grind finely. It is made of roughly equal parts of star anise and Szechuan pepper, with half parts each of fennel, cloves, and cinnamon or cassia.

tabil

The word tabil means "coriander" in Arabic, but in its native Tunisia it can also mean a combination of spices, at least in the context of cuisine. Little known outside Tunisia, this delicious and unusual blend of coriander, caraway, garlic, and chili is one of my favorites. Far less hot than Harissa (see page 59), it nonetheless sparks couscous admirably. In Tunisia the spices are spread out in the hot sun and dried in a matter of hours. In more moderate climates the oven is a better bet.

2 oz. coriander seeds
½ oz. caraway seeds
2-3 cloves garlic, finely chopped
¼ teaspoon chili powder

Pound the coriander and caraway seeds roughly in a mortar, just enough to break them up, then spread them out on a cookie sheet and place it in the coolest preheated oven — 225°F — for about 30 minutes, to dry. Turn off the oven and leave the seeds in it to cool, then pour them into a small spice mill with the garlic and process until reduced to a coarse powder. Add the chili powder, process briefly to mix, then pour the mixture into a small jar and close tightly. Tabil can be kept for 2–3 months, preferably under refrigeration.

Makes 2¾ oz.

English pickling spice

Here is another English convention: a set formula for spices considered best for making pickles. Most often bought ready-made, pickling spice usually consists of cloves, nutmeg, mace, cinnamon, and peppercorns, with optional additions of ginger, allspice, and mustard seeds. I prefer to use individual spices, depending on the main ingredient of the pickle. For fruit, I use a mixture of cinnamon, cloves, and allspice, simmered in white wine vinegar, with added sugar. For meat and fish, I use allspice with black peppercorns. Since pickling spices are to be simmered in liquid, they do not need to be ground. They are usually left whole, sometimes bruised, as in the case of ginger, tied in a square of cheesecloth and later discarded.

shichimi togarishi

Also called "seven spice pepper," "seven flavor spice" or simply "red pepper mix," this Japanese seasoning is a most excellent one, and it is sad that it is not more readily available outside Japan. The usual ingredients are crushed red pepper flakes, coarsely ground sansho berries, dried rind of a mandarin orange or tangerine, poppy seeds, little flakes of nori (a green seaweed sold in sheets), white sesame seeds, and hemp seeds. The resulting blend is an aromatic, tangy seasoning, gingery brown in color and fairly hot. It is mostly used as a condiment, to be placed on the table, for seasoning noodles, soups, and rice dishes.

English mixed spice

This is sometimes called "pudding spice," because it has always been used for seasoning sweet dishes, such as plum pudding, fruit-cakes, and mincemeat. For the past 300 years the English have been very conservative in their use of spices, using ginger for gingerbread, nutmeg for bread sauce, and so on. A mixture of aromatic spices, usually cinnamon, cloves, nutmeg, ginger, and/or allspice, was deemed best in baked, boiled, and steamed puddings, cakes, and cookies. A satisfactory mixture can be made by weighing equal parts of each ingredient. Start with them whole rather than ground, except in the case of nutmeg, which is too hard to grind at home. Grind the others in an electric mill and mix with the nutmeg, then store in an airtight jar.

I prefer to use specific spices in different proportions for each dish. Failing that, I use allspice for English puddings and fruitcakes.

ras el hanout

This is probably the most complex spice mixture to be found anywhere. As made in Morocco, anything up to 26 spices may be used. In Fès vu par sa cuisine (Rabat, 1958), Madame Guineaudeau, a Frenchwoman who lived in Fès for over 30 years, lists the spices that are used in ras el hanout and those that are not; both come to 26. The Fès version is the most complex, and the spices are among the more exotic, including belladonna and cubebs, monk's pepper, and coeurs des roses. Some are aphrodisiac. In Tunisia the mixture is simpler, being reduced to a combination of cinnamon, cloves, cubebs, coeurs des roses, and black peppercorns. Few people make their own, as it is hardly worth the effort of buying all the different ingredients and pounding. Ras el hanout is used with lamb and game, with rice and couscous, and in a sweet called majoun.

recipes

Press 2–3 cloves into a large onion and use to flavor soups, stews, and stocks.

soups

chilled eggplant soup

This unusual and delicious soup is best made a day in advance because the flavors develop while resting.

1 Broil the eggplants and pepper until they have blackened evenly all over. The pepper will take about 20 minutes, the eggplants 30–40 minutes, depending on size. Remove them from the broiler and leave to cool. When they are cool enough to handle, scrape away the skins and discard the stalks and seeds. Chop the eggplants and pepper and put them in a food processor with the sliced scallions, olive oil, lime or lemon juice, ginger, salt, and black pepper. Process until blended, then add the cold chicken stock and process again. Then add most of the yogurt, keeping back about 3 tablespoons for the final garnish. Process once more, adding more salt and pepper as needed, then chill overnight.

2 To serve, beat with a whisk, then pour into individual bowls. Garnish each with ½ tablespoon of thin yogurt drizzled over the top, and a sprinkling of finely chopped cilantro leaves.

Serves 6

2 eggplants
1 large red pepper
1 bunch scallions, sliced
4 tablespoons olive oil
2 tablespoons lime or lemon juice
1 teaspoon ground ginger
1⅞ cups cold chicken stock
⅞ cup thin yogurt
sea salt and black pepper
1 tablespoon finely chopped cilantro leaves (optional), to garnish

beef consommé
with strips of sirloin steak

1½ lb. shin of beef, cubed

some beef or veal bones, such as
  knuckle of veal

1 onion, halved

1 leek, halved

1 carrot, halved

1 celery stalk, halved

3 sprigs parsley

1 bay leaf

10 black peppercorns

1 sirloin steak, about 6 oz.

6 oz. thin egg noodles, Italian or
  Chinese

To garnish:

1 red chili pepper, deseeded and cut
  in thin rings

½ bunch watercress, leaves and
  tender stalks only

1 Start 1 day in advance. Put the beef and bones into a pressure cooker or deep pan. Add 7½ cups cold water and bring very slowly to a boil. As it approaches boiling point, start to skim frequently until the surface is clear. Then pour in ⅝ cup cold water to compensate for what has been lost. Add the flavoring vegetables, herbs, and peppercorns. Simmer for 1 hour under pressure or 3 hours in an ordinary pan, covered. Strain and leave to cool, then chill in the refrigerator overnight.

2 Next day remove the fat and measure the stock. You should have about 6¼ cups; if more, reduce by fast boiling.

3 To serve, cook the steak briefly on a ridged cast-iron broiler pan on top of the heat, or under the broiler, so that it is still rare in the center. Cook the noodles in boiling water for 2 minutes or until tender, then drain and leave in a bowl of hot water until needed. Cut the steak in strips about ¼ inch wide. Reheat the soup. Divide the noodles between 6 bowls and lay 3–4 strips of beef over them. Ladle the hot soup into the bowls, adding a few chili rings and 3 sprigs watercress to each one. Serve immediately.

Serves 6

chicken broth
with ginger dumplings

If you can lay your hands on a beef marrow bone or knuckle of veal, remove the marrow and use it to make extra-light dumplings.

1 chicken carcass or 1½ lb. chicken wings

1 beef marrow bone or knuckle of veal (if available)

1 large onion, cut in 4

2 leeks, cut in chunks

2 carrots, cut in chunks

2 celery stalks, cut in chunks

1 bay leaf

½ tablespoon sea salt

12 black peppercorns

3 stalks lemon grass, roughly crushed

3 slices fresh root ginger, roughly crushed

1 whole red chili

Ginger Dumplings (see page 173), to garnish

1 Start 1 day in advance. Put the chicken carcass or wings in a pressure cooker or deep pan. If you have managed to get a marrow bone or veal knuckle, remove the marrow and reserve it for the dumplings. Add the bones to the chicken and cover with 5 cups cold water. Bring slowly to a boil, skimming frequently as it nears boiling point. (Skimming is necessary only if beef or veal bones are included.) When the surface is clear, add the flavoring vegetables, bay leaf, and seasonings. Screw down the lid of the pressure cooker and cook for 1 hour, or for 3 hours in an ordinary pan, covered. Strain the stock and let it cool, then chill it overnight.

2 Next day remove all fat from the surface. You should have about 4⅜ cups bouillon. Put it in a pan with the lemon grass, ginger, and chili. Reheat slowly, then cover and leave it to infuse while you make the dumplings.

3 Shortly before serving, reheat the soup and discard the lemon grass, ginger, and chili. When the dumplings are ready, ladle the soup into bowls and then put 2–3 dumplings in to each serving bowl.

Note: As a shortcut, you may use any good chicken stock, bought or made at home, as the soup base; simply heat it with lemon grass, ginger, and chili, as above, to flavor it.

Serves 4 to 6

celery soup with cumin

This delicious and unusual soup is based on one I had years ago when staying at the Bristol Cancer Help Center.

1 Toast the cumin and celery seeds in a dry skillet over gentle heat for about 45 seconds, shaking the pan a few times. Then pour them into a small mill and grind, or pound in a mortar.

2 Cook the chopped onion gently in the sunflower oil for 5 minutes, then add the chopped celery, cumin, and celery seeds, and continue to cook for another 10 minutes. Then add the lentils and the heated stock. Bring to a boil and cook for 20 minutes, or until the lentils are soft.

3 Cool slightly, then blend in a food processor with the yogurt, adding the soy sauce and salt and pepper to taste. This excellent soup may be served warm, at room temperature, or chilled.

Serves 6 to 8

2 teaspoons cumin seeds

1 teaspoon celery seeds

1 onion, chopped

3 tablespoons sunflower oil

1 head celery, inner part only, chopped

2 cups red (split) lentils

6¼ cups light chicken stock, heated

2¼ cups yogurt

1 tablespoon light soy sauce

salt and black pepper

crème sénégale

1 Start 1 day in advance. Bring the chicken stock to a boil, drop in the chicken breast, and simmer gently for 8 minutes. Lift out the chicken and leave to cool.

2 Melt the butter, then add the flour and the spices, and cook over gentle heat for 3 minutes, stirring. Then add the chicken stock, bring back to a boil and simmer for another 3–4 minutes. Remove from the heat, stir in the cream and lemon juice, and add salt and black pepper to taste. Stand the pan in a sink half full of cold water and leave to cool, stirring from time to time to prevent a skin from forming.

3 Then dice the chicken breast, discarding the skin and any bone, and stir into the soup. Chill overnight. To serve, spoon into chilled bowls, dividing the pieces of chicken evenly between them. Sprinkle a little cayenne over each bowl.

Serves 6

3¾ cups good chicken stock (see page 73)

1 chicken breast

2 tablespoons butter

2 tablespoons all-purpose flour

1 teaspoon ground cumin

1 teaspoon ground coriander

½ teaspoon ground turmeric

⅝ cup light cream

1 tablespoon lemon juice

salt and black pepper

a little cayenne, to garnish

chicken noodle soup
with chili oil

1 Start several hours or 1 day in advance. Put the chicken in a deep pot with the flavoring vegetables. Add the bay leaves, sea salt, and black peppercorns, then pour on enough cold water to cover the thighs of the chicken. Bring to a boil and simmer gently for 1¼ hours or until the meat is cooked. Then take out the chicken, cut the flesh off the bones, and put the carcass back in the pot. Bring back to a boil and cook for 1 hour, then strain.

2 Remove the fat from the surface and put the soup back in a clean pan with the chopped leek, carrot, and celery. Bring back to a boil and cook over moderate heat for 25 minutes, then add the zucchinis and cook for another 5 minutes. Shake in the soup pasta — I use rice-shaped pasta called *risoni* or the slightly larger *orzi*, or small squares — and cook for another 5 minutes or until it is done.

3 In the meantime cut the chicken into neat pieces, and make the chili oil. Put the hot red pepper flakes in a small pan, cover with the oil and warm very gently. Allow it to heat through for 10 minutes without approaching boiling point. Add to the soup with the chicken, reheat and allow to stand for at least 15 minutes before serving. This soup improves on keeping, and is even better the second day.

Serves 6

3½–4 lb. chicken
flavoring vegetables, such as onion, carrot, and celery, trimmings of those you will use in the soup itself
2 bay leaves
½ tablespoon sea salt
8 black peppercorns
1 large leek, neatly chopped
1 large carrot, neatly chopped
1 celery stalk, neatly chopped
2 zucchinis, neatly chopped
¾ cup soup pasta

Chili oil:
½ tablespoon hot red pepper flakes
2 tablespoons extra virgin olive oil

Put the stock in a pan and add the carrot, leek, and beet. Bring slowly to a boil and simmer for 10 minutes, then add the zucchinis, peppers, and chili. Bring back to a boil and simmer for another 10 minutes, then add the peas and simmer again for 4–5 minutes, adding salt and pepper to taste. Serve hot, in bowls, liberally sprinkled with chopped chervil.

Note: This is also excellent chilled in hot weather. It may be eaten quite plain, with chopped chervil, or with a spoonful of yogurt added to each bowl and the chervil sprinkled over it.

Serves 6

5 cups chicken stock
I cup diced carrot
I cup diced leek
I cup peeled and diced cooked beet
I large zucchini, diced
I cup diced yellow or red pepper
I red or green chili, deseeded and
** finely chopped**
½ cup shelled peas
sea salt and black pepper
4 tablespoons chopped chervil, to
** garnish**

consommé with mixed vegetables

spiced zucchini soup

This is a delicate soup, very mildly spiced, best eaten not too hot.

1 Cook the sliced onion in the butter and oil until pale golden, about 6 minutes, adding the spices halfway through. Then add the zucchinis and cook for 4 minutes. Pour in the heated stock, adding salt and pepper to taste, and cook gently for 20 minutes; then leave to cool.

2 When it has cooled somewhat, pour the soup into a food processor and process to a rough purée — it should not be smooth. Then add the yogurt and process again. Reheat gently, without allowing the soup to come too near boiling point or the yogurt will separate. Serve in bowls, sprinkled with cilantro leaves.

Serves 6

1 onion, sliced

2 tablespoons butter

2 tablespoons sunflower oil

$\frac{1}{2}$ tablespoon ground cumin

$\frac{1}{2}$ tablespoon ground coriander

4 large zucchinis, trimmed and coarsely chopped

3$\frac{3}{4}$ cups chicken stock, heated

$\frac{5}{8}$ cup yogurt

salt and black pepper

2 tablespoons chopped cilantro leaves, to garnish

saffron soup

This rustic and delicious soup is based on a French provincial dish.

1 Cook the sliced leeks slowly in the oil for 5 minutes, adding the garlic toward the end. Then put in the potatoes and tomatoes, thyme, saffron, salt, and pepper. Stir for 2–3 minutes, then pour on the heated stock and bring to a boil.

2 Cover and simmer gently for 25 minutes, adding more salt and pepper if needed. Serve in bowls, generously sprinkled with chopped parsley.

Serves 4

3 leeks, sliced

3 tablespoons olive oil

3 garlic cloves, sliced

8 oz. waxy potatoes, peeled and thickly sliced

1$\frac{1}{4}$ cups skinned and coarsely chopped tomatoes

3 sprigs thyme, fresh or dried

$\frac{1}{4}$ teaspoon powdered saffron

3$\frac{3}{4}$ cups chicken stock, heated

salt and black pepper

4 tablespoons chopped flat-leaf parsley, to garnish

curried fruit soup

3 shallots, finely chopped

3 tablespoons sunflower oil

I garlic clove, finely chopped

I red chili, deseeded and finely
chopped

I teaspoon ground coriander

I teaspoon ground cumin

½ teaspoon ground turmeric

½ teaspoon ground ginger

I teaspoon sea salt

3¾ cups chicken stock

½ small melon, cut in cubes

2 peaches or 3 apricots, pitted,
skinned, and cut in cubes

2 bananas, thickly sliced

2 kiwi fruit, peeled and thickly sliced

2 tablespoons orange juice

2 tablespoons lime or lemon juice

⅞ cup thin yogurt

I tablespoon finely chopped chives
or cilantro leaves, to garnish

Best made a day in advance, this excellent soup improves immeasurably on keeping.

1 Cook the shallots gently in the oil for 3 minutes, then add the garlic, chili, spices, and sea salt. Cook for another 3–4 minutes, stirring often. Heat the chicken stock and add to the spice mixture, stirring until blended. Simmer for 5 minutes, then remove from the heat and stir in the prepared fruit. Leave to cool, then pour into the food processor, adding the fruit juices and most of the yogurt, keeping back about 3 tablespoons for the garnish. Process until blended — it does not need to be absolutely smooth — then chill for several hours or overnight.

2 To serve, pour into individual bowls and swirl a little thin yogurt over the surface. Sprinkle with a few finely chopped chives or cilantro leaves.

Serves 6

2 lb. mixed white fish: monkfish,
   gray mullet, conger eel, cod, and
   so on, with their bones
1 onion, halved
1 carrot, halved
1 celery stalk, halved
1 bay leaf
2 tablespoons olive oil
1 leek, sliced
1 garlic clove, finely chopped
2 tomatoes, skinned and finely
   chopped
2 sprigs fennel
2 inch strip orange peel
½ teaspoon powdered saffron
¼ teaspoon cayenne
2–3 shakes Tabasco Sauce
salt and black pepper

To garnish:
18 thin slices French bread, dried in
   the oven
Rouille (see page 191)
freshly grated Parmesan cheese

1 Fillet the fish and put the bones in a deep pot with the onion, carrot, and celery. Cover with 5 cups of water, adding the bay leaf, salt, and pepper. Bring to a boil slowly, skimming as it nears boiling point. Boil gently, half covered, for 30 minutes, then strain and reserve the stock; discard the bones and vegetables.

2 Heat the oil in a pan and cook the leek for 3 minutes. Add the garlic and cook for 2 minutes; add the tomatoes and cook for another 2 minutes. Bury the fennel and orange peel in the vegetables. Divide the fish into firm (monkfish, conger eel, and so on) and softer fish (gray mullet and so on). Cut into small pieces; lay the firmer ones on top of the vegetables. Cover the pan and cook gently for 4 minutes, then add the fish stock. Bring to a boil and cook briskly for 10 minutes; lower the heat, add the softer fish, simmer for 5 minutes. Turn off the heat, add the saffron, cayenne, and Tabasco. Let stand, covered, for 5–10 minutes before serving.

3 To serve, pour into a large tureen or into individual soup bowls. Place dishes of dried bread, rouille, and freshly grated Parmesan on the table. Each person then spreads the rouille or the grated cheese on the bread and floats it in the soup.

Note: If using saffron threads, toast them first by holding them in a large metal spoon over a low heat for 30 seconds, then pound in a mortar. Pour 2 tablespoons boiling water over the pounded saffron and leave for 10 minutes to infuse. Then add to the soup along with the cayenne and Tabasco.

Serves 6

fish soup with rouille

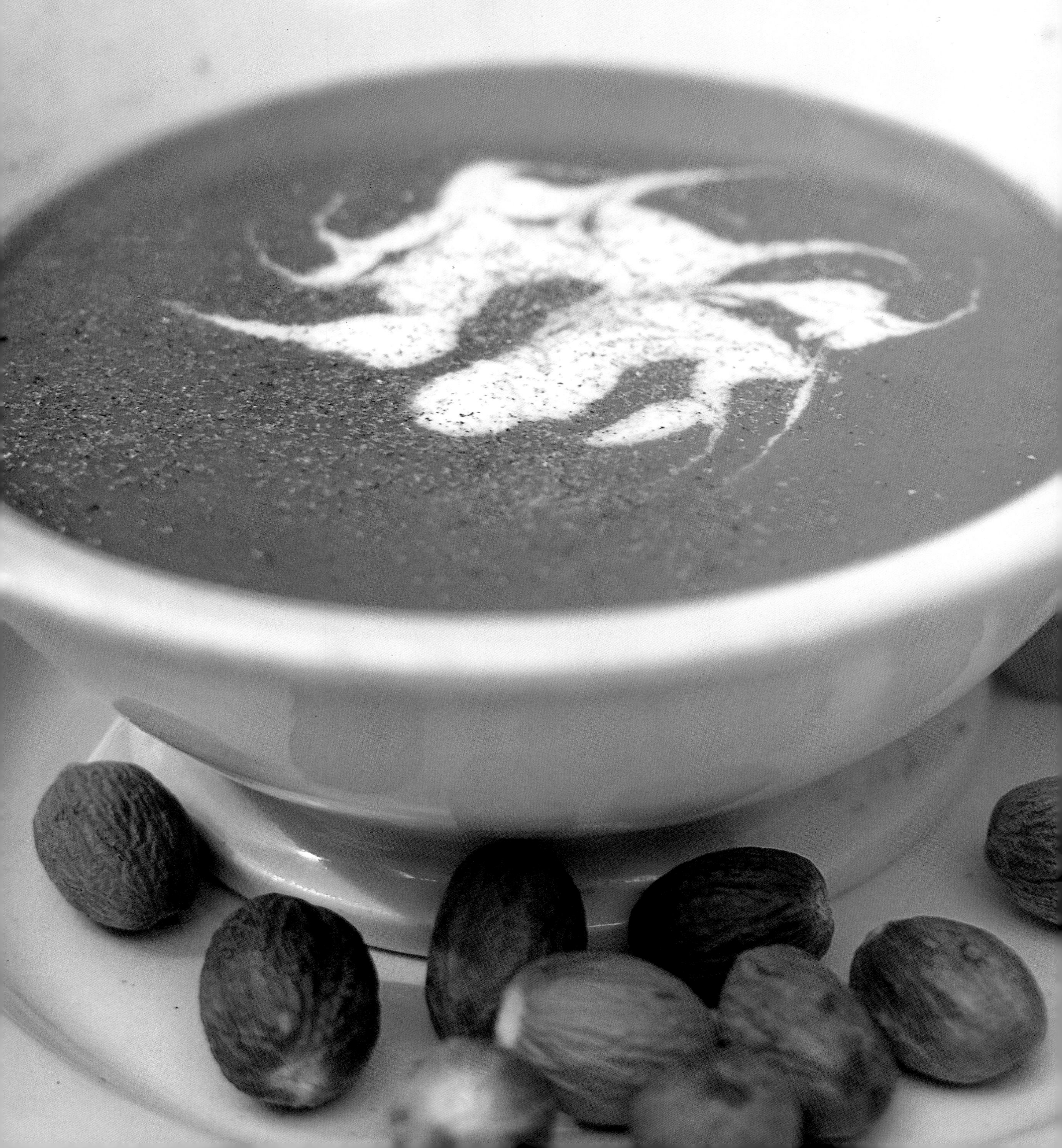

spinach soup
with nutmeg or ginger

1 cup finely chopped onion

2 tablespoons butter

1 tablespoon sunflower oil

8 oz. spinach

1¼ cups peeled and diced potato

3¾ cups chicken stock, heated

sea salt and black pepper

To garnish:

6 tablespoons cream (any thickness) or 6 tablespoons yogurt

freshly grated nutmeg or ground ginger

1 Cook the chopped onion in the butter and sunflower oil for 5 minutes, then add the spinach and cook for another 5 minutes. Add the diced potato and cook all together for 3–4 minutes, stirring; then pour on the heated stock and bring to a boil. Cook gently for 25 minutes, half covered; add salt and pepper to taste.

2 Cool for a little while before puréeing in the food processor. Reheat to serve. Pour into individual bowls, swirl cream or yogurt into each bowl, and then sprinkle with a little freshly grated nutmeg or ground ginger.

Serves 4

cold curried onion soup

1 Cook the sliced onions slowly in the oil, allowing at least 12 minutes for them to soften without browning. Warm the saffron threads gently in a large metal spoon or soup ladle held over a low heat for 30 seconds. Then pound the threads in a mortar and pour 1 tablespoon of the heated chicken stock over them. Leave for 5 minutes to infuse.

2 When the onions have softened, stir in the curry powder and the flour and cook gently, stirring, for 3 minutes. Add the saffron liquid and cook for 1 minute, then add the rest of the heated stock, with the hot red pepper flakes, salt, and pepper. Bring to a boil, stirring; then lower the heat and simmer gently for 15 minutes. Allow to cool completely, then pour into a food processor and purée with the yogurt, lime, or lemon juice and cilantro. Chill for several hours or overnight.

Serves 6

1 lb. onions, sliced
4 tablespoons sunflower oil
½ teaspoon saffron threads
4¼ cups light chicken stock, heated
1½ tablespoons light curry powder
2 tablespoons all-purpose flour
¼ teaspoon hot red pepper flakes
⅝ cup yogurt
2 tablespoon lime or lemon juice
4 tablespoons cilantro leaves, roughly chopped
salt and black pepper

pea soup with cumin

1 Drop the potatoes into the cold stock and bring to a boil. Simmer for 15 minutes or until soft. Melt the butter in a sauté pan and cook the chopped shallots for 3 minutes, adding the cumin halfway through. Then add the snow peas or sugar snap peas and cook for another 5 minutes. Pour the contents of the pea pan onto the potatoes, bring back to a boil and simmer for 5 minutes.

2 Push through a coarse food mill — do not use a food processor, as there may be stringy elements, which need to be withheld. Then pour the purée back into a clean pan, add the sugar and seasoning, and reheat. Pour into bowls to serve, with 1 tablespoon cream swirled into each one.

Note: For a cold soup, make as above and chill for several hours or overnight. Add the cream only just before serving.

Serves 6

8 oz. potatoes, peeled and thickly sliced
4¼ cups light chicken stock
3 tablespoons butter
3 shallots, finely chopped
2 teaspoons cumin seeds
12 oz. snow peas or sugar snap peas, cut in 2–3 pieces
¼ teaspoon sugar
⅝ cup light cream
sea salt and black pepper

oriental fish soup

1 lb. raw tiger shrimps or king
   shrimps, unshelled
5 cups chicken stock
1 inch square fresh root ginger,
   crushed
2 stalks lemon grass
¼ teaspoon dried galangal or ground
   ginger
2 green chilies, deseeded and sliced
   in thin rings

To garnish:
1½ oz. thin egg noodles
3 tablespoons lime or lemon juice
rind of ½ lime, cut in long, thin strips
   (optional)
2 tablespoons cilantro leaves, torn

1 Shell the shrimps and drop the heads, tails, and shells into the cold chicken stock. Heat slowly, adding the crushed ginger, lemon grass, and galangal or ground ginger. When boiling point is reached, half-cover the pan and simmer for just 20 minutes. Strain through cheesecloth into a clean pan, add the sliced chilies and bring back to a boil. Drop in the shelled shrimps and cook gently for 6 minutes, then remove from the heat. Cool for 8–10 minutes.

2 Cook the egg noodles for 2–3 minutes in lightly salted boiling water. Drain the noodles and divide them between the soup bowls. Add the lime or lemon juice to the soup and pour it over the noodles, dividing the shrimps evenly between the bowls. Scatter the strips of lime peel and the cilantro leaves over the surface, and then serve.

Serves 6

potato soup with celery seeds

3 tablespoons sunflower oil
1 tablespoon celery seeds
1 onion, chopped
1 lb. potatoes, peeled and diced
2½ cups chicken stock, heated
2½ cups low-fat milk, heated
salt and black pepper
2 tablespoons chopped chives, to
   garnish

I have based this soup on one in Oded Schwartz's book In Search of Plenty *(Kyle Cathie, 1992). Caraway or cumin seeds, or black onion seeds, may be substituted for the celery seeds.*

1 Heat the oil in a heavy pan and fry the celery seeds for a moment or two, then add the chopped onion and cook gently until it starts to color. Then add the potatoes and the chicken stock. Bring toward boiling point, then add the milk, and salt and pepper to taste. Simmer gently for 30 minutes or until the potatoes are soft.

2 Set aside and leave to cool. Process the cooled mixture to a lumpy purée in the food processor, and adjust the seasoning. Chill for a few hours or overnight, before serving in bowls, sprinkled with chopped chives.

Serves 6

Sprinkling cracked black pepper on a soft-boiled egg adds greatly to the flavor.

eggs

hard-boiled eggs
with dukkah

One of my favorite dishes for a solitary meal is as follows: 2 very fresh eggs, boiled for exactly 12 minutes and cooled for 3–4 minutes in cold water before shelling, with 2 thick slices of whole grain bread, some unsalted butter, and a small dish of Dukkah (see page 62). Dip the warm eggs in the dukkah before eating; the dukkah may also be spread liberally on the bread and butter. A sustaining meal, it is quickly made and very enjoyable.

celery seed eggs

1 Shell the eggs, cut in half and remove the yolks. Slice the whites quite thickly and lay them in a shallow fireproof dish. Sprinkle half the celery seeds over the egg whites.

2 Melt the butter, add the flour, and cook for 1 minute, stirring. Add the heated milk and stir until blended, then simmer gently for 3 minutes, stirring now and then. Now add the grated Parmesan, stirring until smooth, and season well with sea salt and black pepper. Pour half the hot sauce over the egg whites, then rub the yolks through a strainer and scatter most of them over the sauce, reserving 1½ tablespoons. Spread the remaining celery seeds over the egg yolks, and pour the rest of the sauce over all. Sprinkle the reserved egg yolk over the top, and bake in a preheated oven, 375°F, for 10 minutes. If the dish has been freshly made and is still hot, this should be long enough. Alternatively, make in advance and reheat at 325°F, for 30 minutes, loosely covered with foil for the first 15 minutes. Sprinkle with parsley before serving.

Serves 4 as a first course, or 2 to 3 as a light main dish with a green salad.

6 eggs, hard-boiled
½ tablespoon celery seeds

White sauce:
¼ cup butter
3 tablespoons all-purpose flour
1⅞ cups milk, heated
3 tablespoons freshly grated
  Parmesan cheese
sea salt and black pepper
1 tablespoon very finely chopped
  flat-leaf parsley, to garnish

curried eggs

8 eggs
1 onion
¼ cup butter
1 tablespoon light curry powder
1 tablespoon all-purpose flour
1⅞ cups chicken or vegetable stock,
  heated
⅝ cup light cream
1½ tablespoons orange juice
1½ tablespoons lemon juice
½ cup coarsely chopped almonds
1½ tablespoons finely chopped
  cilantro leaves, to garnish

This is an English dish, as opposed to an Indian one, hence the use of curry powder. It is good nonetheless.

1 Cook the eggs in lightly salted boiling water for 12 minutes, then drain and cool in a bowl of cold water. Cook the onion gently in the butter until golden, about 8 minutes. Then add the curry powder and flour, and cook for another 2 minutes. Add the hot stock, stir until blended, and simmer for 15 minutes. Then stir in the cream, the orange and lemon juices, and the chopped almonds.

2 Shell the eggs, cut them into quarters, then cut each quarter across in half. Fold them into the sauce, reheat gently, and tip into a serving dish. Scatter the chopped cilantro on top, and serve with plain boiled rice and some chutney.

Serves 4 as a light main course.

eggs on spinach purée
with tomato sauce

This makes an excellent first course for a summer lunch or dinner. If you like a mixture of temperatures, as I do, you may leave the tomato sauce cold. If you prefer everything hot, be careful not to let the sauce get too hot or you will lose its fresh taste.

6 eggs
Spinach Purée with Mace
  (see page 154)
Fresh Tomato Sauce (see page 185)

1 Bring a pan of lightly salted water to a boil and lower in the eggs. Cook gently for 5 minutes, lift them out and lower into a bowl of cold water. As soon as they are cool enough to handle, shell them carefully to avoid breaking them.

2 Spoon the hot spinach purée into bowls. Place an egg in each one and cover each egg with 2 tablespoons tomato sauce, at your preferred temperature. Serve as soon as possible after assembling.

Serves 6

fried eggs
on sun-dried tomato purée

Provided you have some cornbread made or polenta already cooked, and some sun-dried tomato paste on hand, this is a quick and very delicious snack.

4 rounds Cornbread (see page 201) or Polenta (see page 178)
1 dried chili, deseeded and stalk removed
6 tablespoons sun-dried tomato paste
4 eggs
butter for frying
sea salt and black pepper

1 Have the cornbread or polenta cut in neat circles or squares about ½ inch thick. Cover the dried chili with 4 tablespoons boiling water and leave for 20 minutes. Then lift out the chili and chop; purée with half the soaking water in a small mill or coffee grinder. Stir into the sun-dried tomato paste and mix well.

2 Grill the cornbread or polenta on a ridged cast-iron broiler pan on top of the heat until nicely striped with brown, or cook under the broiler, and then lay on individual plates and top with the tomato and chili paste. Keep them warm while you fry the eggs in the butter. Place 1 egg on each prepared bed and serve at once.

Serves 4 with a green salad.

egg mayonnaise on spinach

A chili-accented mayonnaise makes a good contrast to the bland egg, lifting this excellent dish out of the ordinary.

1 Make the Chili Mayonnaise as instructed. Boil the eggs in salted water for 12 minutes, then cool in a bowl of cold water. Place the spinach in a large pan of lightly salted boiling water and cook for 4–5 minutes, depending on whether it is tender summer or coarser winter spinach. Drain very well, squeezing out all the moisture in a colander with the back of a wooden spoon.

2 Make a bed of spinach, still slightly warm, on a flat platter, seasoning it with sea salt and black pepper. Shell the eggs, cut them in half and place them on the spinach, then spoon the mayonnaise over all. Serve soon after making.

Serves 4 as a fairly substantial first course.

Chili Mayonnaise (see page 183)
6 eggs
2 lb. spinach
sea salt and black pepper

scrambled eggs
on smoky pepper purée

1 Make the cornbread 1 day in advance; omit chili. Bake it in a small loaf pan.

2 Next day prepare the purée. Broil the peppers and tomatoes until blackened. Skin and chop them. Soak the smoked chili in 4 tablespoons boiling water for 20 minutes, chop roughly, and purée in a small food mill or coffee grinder with its water. Cook the garlic in the oil for 1 minute; do not to let it burn. Add the peppers and tomatoes and cook for 10 minutes. Add the chili purée, salt, and pepper and cook for 5 minutes. Leave to cool, then purée in the food processor.

3 Broil the cornbread on both sides on a ridged cast-iron broiler pan on top of the heat. When the bread is crisp and golden, lay 1 slice on each plate and cover each with 2 tablespoons of the pepper purée. Melt the butter in a pan, pour in the eggs and scramble. Pile the eggs on top of the purée and scatter cilantro over each.

Note: The cornbread can be replaced by squares of Polenta (see page 178) made in advance and browned as above; or thick slices of pugliese bread, broiled as above; or 4 inch sections of ciabatta or broad baguette, split and broiled as above.

Serves 4 as a first course, or as a light main dish accompanied by thin slices of prosciutto and a green salad.

4 slices Cornbread (see page 201),
½ inch thick
1 tablespoon butter
5 eggs, beaten
1 tablespoon finely chopped cilantro
leaves, to garnish

Pepper purée:
1 large red pepper
1 large yellow pepper
4 large tomatoes
1 smoked dried chili, halved and
deseeded
2 garlic cloves, finely chopped
2 tablespoons light olive oil
sea salt and black pepper

oeufs soubises

1 Cook the sliced onions slowly in the butter without allowing them to brown; it will take at least 10 minutes for them to soften. Add the flour, stirring, then add the heated stock and the cream. Bring to a boil, stirring, then lower the heat and simmer gently for 15 minutes, half covered. Add the grated cheese and stir until it has melted smoothly. Then add the sea salt and black pepper to taste, and the ground mace.

2 Shell the eggs and cut in halves; fold them gently into the sauce. Butter a shallow fireproof dish, pour in the eggs and sauce, and brown quickly under the broiler.

Serves 4 as a first course, or 3 as a light main dish with a green salad.

2 large onions, halved and thickly
sliced
3 tablespoons butter
2 tablespoons all-purpose flour
1⅞ cups chicken stock, heated
⅝ cup light cream
¼ cup grated Gruyère cheese
¼ teaspoon ground mace
6 eggs, hard-boiled
sea salt and black pepper

eggs in mustard sauce

This makes a delicate dish, good for eating early, before the theater, or late at night.

1 Make the mustard sauce in advance, keeping back a little of the chopped dill weed. Cook the rice in plenty of lightly salted boiling water for about 10 minutes or until tender; drain well. Put the eggs in a pan of lightly salted cold water, bring to a boil and cook for 12 minutes; then put in cold water.

2 When they are cool enough to handle, remove the shells. Divide the rice between 4 bowls and place 1 egg in each bowl. Reheat the sauce briefly, without allowing it to boil, and pour over the eggs. Sprinkle with the remaining chopped dill weed and serve immediately, with spoons and forks. Alternatively, it may be served in one shallow dish, and eaten with knives and forks.

Serves 4 as a light main course, to be followed by a green salad.

Hot Mustard Sauce (see page 188), made with chicken stock
¾ cup white basmati rice
6 eggs

saffron baked eggs

1 Put the saffron in a large metal spoon or soup ladle and warm it over low heat for about 30 seconds, moving it from side to side. Then pound it in a mortar. Pour 1½ teaspoons almost-boiling water over it and leave for 5 minutes to infuse. Then pour on the cream and mix well with the saffron.

2 Butter 6 ramekins, break an egg into each one, and sprinkle with sea salt and pepper. Place the ramekins in a roasting pan with hot water coming halfway up their sides. Bake in a preheated oven, 325°F, for about 10 minutes, or until the whites are semi-opaque. Then warm the saffron cream and pour 1½ tablespoons over each egg. Put back in the oven for another 2–3 minutes, then serve immediately.

Serves 6 as a first course.

½ teaspoon saffron threads
1¼ cups light cream
6 eggs
sea salt and black pepper

scrambled eggs
with green chilies

Toast the bread, and then butter it lightly, using half the butter. Spread each slice of bread with ½ tablespoon tomato purée, then keep them warm. Melt the remaining butter in a frying pan, add the chilies and cook for 30 seconds, stirring. Then tip in the seasoned, beaten eggs and scramble as usual. Pile on to the toast to serve.

Serves 4 as a light meal with a green salad.

4 slices whole grain bread

¼ cup butter

2 tablespoons tomato purée

2 green chilies, deseeded and cut in thin strips

8 eggs, beaten

sea salt and black pepper

fish

Adding fennel butter to broiled fish steaks gives a subtly spicy taste. To make fennel butter, grind 2 tablespoons lightly toasted fennel seeds in a spice mill and put in a food processor with $\frac{7}{8}$ cup sweet butter, $\frac{1}{2}$ teaspoons sea salt, a few turns of the black-pepper mill, and $\frac{1}{2}$ tablespoon lemon juice. Process until blended, then chill for 1 hour to firm. Form into a roll and wrap in foil. Chill again, or freeze.
To serve, cut in thick slices and lay on broiled fish steaks.

crab rolls with tamarind sauce

These are best made with your own freshly sprouted mung beans, as opposed to pur-chased ones, which are allowed to grow too long. But this means planning ahead, as mung beans take 2½–3 days to sprout to about ½ inch long. Failing this, substitute the same weight of shredded fennel and leek for the sprouts. If using fennel and leek, cut them by hand into thin slivers, like the scallions. I advise buying the filo pastry for this dish in small sheets, 7 x 12 inches. These are easier to handle than the large sheets, which, however, are still the best for making large pies.

1 Trim the scallions down to 1½ inches and split them lengthwise into thin slivers. Heat a wok or deep pan, then add the oil and reheat. When the oil is very hot, put in the scallions and toss for 1 minute; then add the garlic, chili, and ginger. Toss together for 1 minute, then add the bean sprouts, or leek and fennel, and toss for another 1–2 minutes. Now put the crabmeat into the pan, adding the soy sauce. Toss once more for 1 minute, then set aside.

2 Unfold the filo and spread out 1 sheet, keeping the others loosely covered with a damp cloth. Cut the first sheet into strips 6 x 10 inches. Brush each one with melted butter, then lay 1½ tablespoons of the crabmeat filling in the center of each short end. Fold over the sides of the filo to enclose the crabmeat, then roll u p and seal the edges by brushing with more melted butter. Repeat the filling and sealing process with the rest of the filling, making 8 rolls measuring roughly 1½ x 3 ½ inches. Lay the rolls on a greased cookie sheet and bake in a preheated oven, 350°F, for 20 minutes or until golden.

3 While they are baking, make the tamarind sauce. Mix the *sake* or vermouth with the soy sauce, then stir in the tamarind syrup. (If using tamarind purée, it is best to mix the *sake* and soy into this, beating until smooth and straining if nec-essary.) Pour the sauce into tiny dishes and set one by each place.

Note: These crab rolls are also good served with Salsa Fresca (see page 191). In this case, omit the chili in the filling.

Serves 4 as a first course.

2 bunches scallions
2 tablespoons sunflower oil
I garlic clove, finely chopped
I fresh chili, deseeded and finely
 chopped (optional)
2 teaspoons grated fresh ginger
3 cups mung bean sprouts, or
 I cup each shredded fennel
 and leek
¾ cup white crabmeat, flaked
a dash of light soy sauce
about 3 oz. filo pastry
3 tablespoons butter, melted

Tamarind sauce:
4 tablespoons *sake* or dry vermouth
4 tablespoons light soy sauce
I tablespoon Tamarind Syrup (see
 page 222) or 2 teaspoons tamarind
 purée

Ludmilla's cod fish balls

This is a Polish recipe, which uses nutmeg to flavor the delicate fish balls. The fish balls are poached in fish and vegetable stock, and may be served quite plain, with vegetables or with a cream sauce.

Stock:

fish skin, bones, trimmings
1 onion, thickly sliced
1 carrot, thickly sliced
1 leek, thickly sliced
1 celery stalk, thinly sliced
1 bay leaf
1 tablespoon sea salt
8 black peppercorns

Fish balls:

2 oz. dry white bread,
  crusts removed
6 tablespoons milk
1 lb. cod fillet, skinned
  and chopped
2 onions, chopped
1 egg, beaten
½ tablespoon freshly grated nutmeg
sea salt and black pepper

Cream sauce (optional):

⅝ cup fish stock, strained
2 tablespoons butter
1 tablespoon flour
⅝ cup light cream
¼ teaspoon freshly grated nutmeg
1½ tablespoons chopped dill, chervil,
  or flat-leaf parsley
sea salt and black pepper

1 To make the stock, put the fish skin and any other trimmings, the sliced vegetables, bay leaf, and seasonings into a pan and add 3¾ cups, to cover. Bring slowly to a boil and simmer while you make the fish balls.

2 Soak the bread in the milk for 10 minutes, then squeeze out most of the milk, leaving about 2 tablespoons. (You can measure what you squeeze out to calculate this.) Put the chopped fish in the food processor with the chopped onion. Process to a fine hash, then add the soaked bread and process again. Add the beaten egg, nutmeg, salt, and pepper. Process once more, then take out 1 heaped tablespoon at a time and roll lightly on a floured board, with floured hands, to make balls slightly larger than a golf ball. You should have about 15.

3 Shortly before serving, drop the fish balls into the simmering fish stock, cover the pan, and poach gently for 5 minutes. Then lift them out with a slotted spoon.

4 If making a cream sauce, keep the fish balls warm while you strain the stock. In a small pan, melt the butter, add the flour, and then cook for 1 minute, stirring. Then pour on the measured stock, followed by the cream, adding nutmeg, salt, and pepper to taste. Bring to a boil and simmer for 3 minutes, then stir in the chopped herb. Pour the sauce over the fish balls in their dish or serve separately in a sauceboat.

Serves 4 with a green vegetable.

curried cod steaks

with lentils

1 Place the lentils in a pan of water, bring to a boil, and simmer for about 30 minutes or until tender; then drain, reserving the lentil stock.

2 Make the spice mixture by mixing the spices and salt with the flour. Coat the cod steaks with this, patting it on well on both sides. Fry the chopped onion in 2 tablespoons of the oil for 4 minutes, then add the garlic and cumin, and cook for another 2 minutes. Pour the lentils into the pan and stir over low heat for 2–3 minutes, then add 4–6 tablespoons of the lentil stock to moisten, and salt and pepper to taste. Simmer gently for 5 minutes, adding a little more stock if needed.

3 Shortly before serving, heat the remaining sunflower oil in a wide skillet and fry the cod steaks, allowing about 4 minutes on each side. Serve the fried cod steaks with the reheated lentils.

Serves 4

2 cups lentils, washed and
  drained
4 cod steaks, about 1 inch
  thick
1 red onion, chopped
4½ tablespoons sunflower oil
1 garlic clove, chopped
2 tablespoons ground cumin
sea salt and black pepper

Spice mixture:
1 tablespoon ground
  coriander
½ tablespoon ground cumin
1 teaspoon ground turmeric
½ teaspoon ground ginger
½ teaspoon sea salt
2 tablespoons all-purpose
  flour, sifted

lobster roll
with wasabi and ginger

1 Trim the scallions down to 1½ inches and split them lengthwise into thin slivers. Heat a wok or deep pan, then add the oil and reheat. When the oil is very hot, put in the scallions and toss for 1 minute; then add the garlic and ginger. Toss together for 1 minute, then add the fennel and leek and toss for another 1–2 minutes. Now put the chopped lobster into the pan, adding the soy sauce. Toss once more for 1 minute, then set aside.

2 Unfold the filo and spread out 1 sheet, keeping the others loosely covered with a damp cloth. Cut the first sheet into strips 6 x 10 inches. Brush each one with melted butter, then lay 1½ tablespoons of the lobster filling in the center of each short end. Fold over the sides of the filo to enclose the filling, then roll up and seal the edges by brushing with more melted butter. Repeat the process with the rest of the filling, making 8 rolls measuring about 1½ x 3 inches. Lay the rolls on a greased cookie sheet and bake in a preheated oven, 350°F, for 20 minutes or until golden brown.

3 While they are baking, make the wasabi and ginger sauce. Mix the *sake* or vermouth and soy sauce, then stir in the wasabi and ginger. Pour into tiny dishes and set one by each place.

Serves 4

2 bunches scallions
2 tablespoons sunflower oil
I garlic clove, finely chopped
2 teaspoons grated fresh root ginger
I cup shredded fennel
I cup shredded leek
chopped meat of I lb. lobster
a dash of light soy sauce
about 3 oz. filo pastry
3 tablespoons butter, melted

Wasabi and ginger sauce:
4 tablespoons *sake* or dry vermouth
4 tablespoons light soy sauce
½ teaspoon wasabi
½ teaspoon grated fresh root ginger

spicy fish cakes

1 Place the cod on a board and chop roughly by hand, removing any bones that may have been overlooked. Put the fish into a bowl, add the mashed potatoes, and mix well. Cook the scallions in the oil for 1 minute, then add the spices and continue to cook for another 2 minutes. Mix the onions and spices with the fish and potatoes, adding the chopped parsley, and salt and pepper to taste. Form into round cakes; allow about 3 oz. for each. Chill for a few hours or overnight.

2 Shortly before cooking, dip each cake in beaten egg, then in breadcrumbs. Pour a shallow layer, about ½ inch deep, of sunflower oil into a wide skillet and fry the cakes until golden on each side. Serve with Fresh Tomato Sauce (see page 185), made with or without chilies, according to taste.

Note: The same mixture may be made into small round cakes or rolls weighing about ¾ oz. each, for serving with drinks. It makes about 30.

Makes 8 fish cakes; serves 4

1 lb. cod, cooked, boned, and flaked
8 oz. freshly mashed potatoes
1 bunch scallions, sliced
1 tablespoon sunflower oil
1 teaspoon ground coriander
1 teaspoon ground cumin
¼ teaspoon cayenne or chili powder
2 tablespoons chopped flat-
  leaf parsley
1 egg, beaten
dry white breadcrumbs
salt and black pepper
sunflower oil, for frying

shellfish & vegetable
mayonnaise

This is an adaptable dish, easily made with whatever is in season. It is also very pretty and easy to serve. White crabmeat is not easy to buy without the brown, which is too rich for this dish. I usually buy dressed crab, using the brown meat for something else.

1 Make the mayonnaise as directed, using 1 teaspoon chili powder. Steam or boil the asparagus tips or string beans for about 4 minutes or until just tender.

2 On 4 flat plates arrange a mound of white crabmeat or cooked shrimps in one section. Lay the asparagus tips or string beans in another section, then lay out the quartered eggs and the halved tomatoes. In the center, spoon a generous amount of chili mayonnaise. (This may be served separately if preferred.)

Note: The shellfish should be kept chilled until the last moment, but the eggs and vegetables are better served at room temperature. Therefore it is best to assemble everything except the shellfish beforehand, adding them last.

Serves 4 as a first course.

1¼ cups Chili Mayonnaise II (see
  page 183)
20 asparagus tips, or string beans,
  trimmed
1½ cups white crabmeat or cooked
  shrimps
6 eggs, hard-boiled, shelled, and
  quartered
8 yellow or red cherry tomatoes,
  halved horizontally

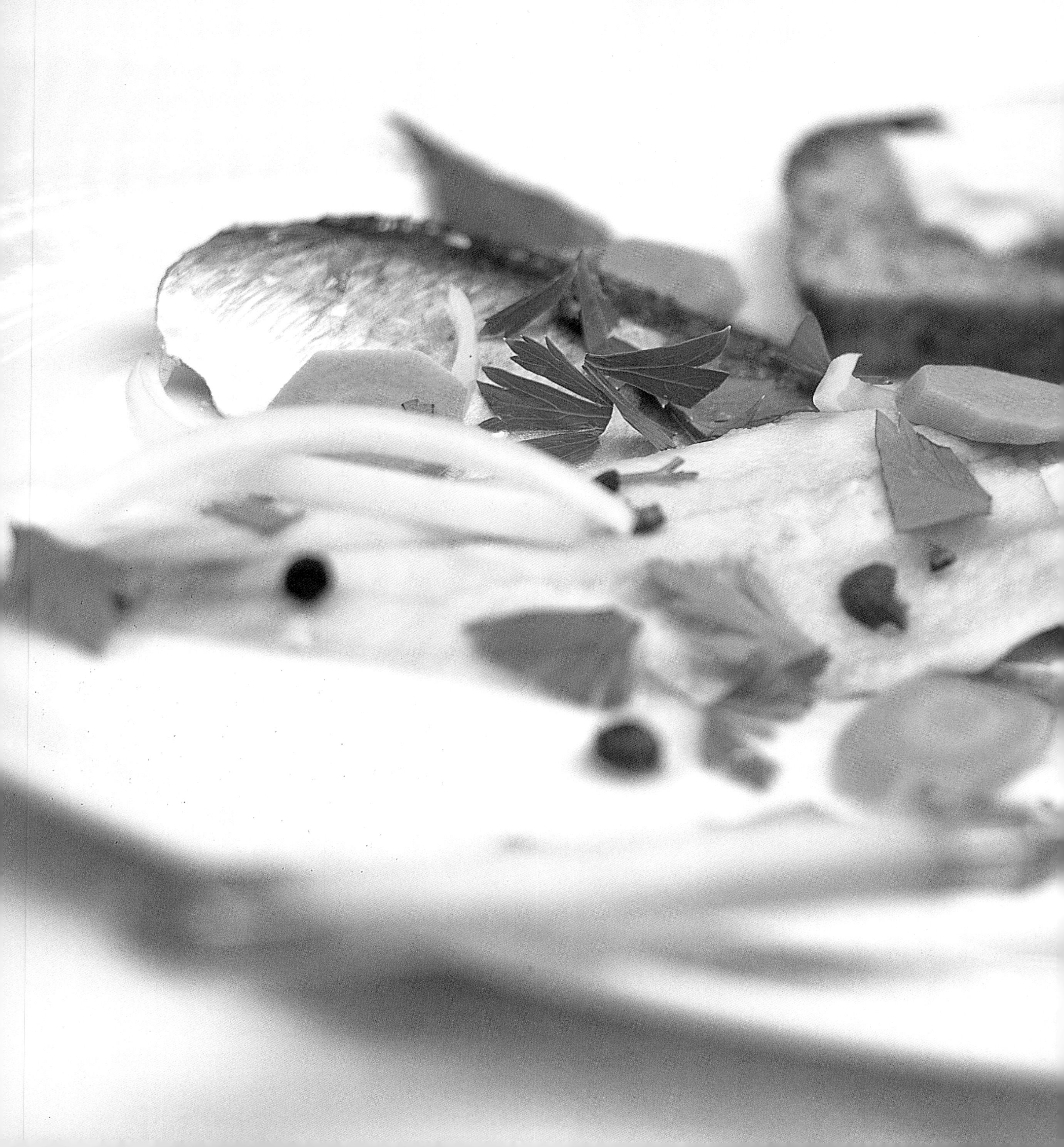

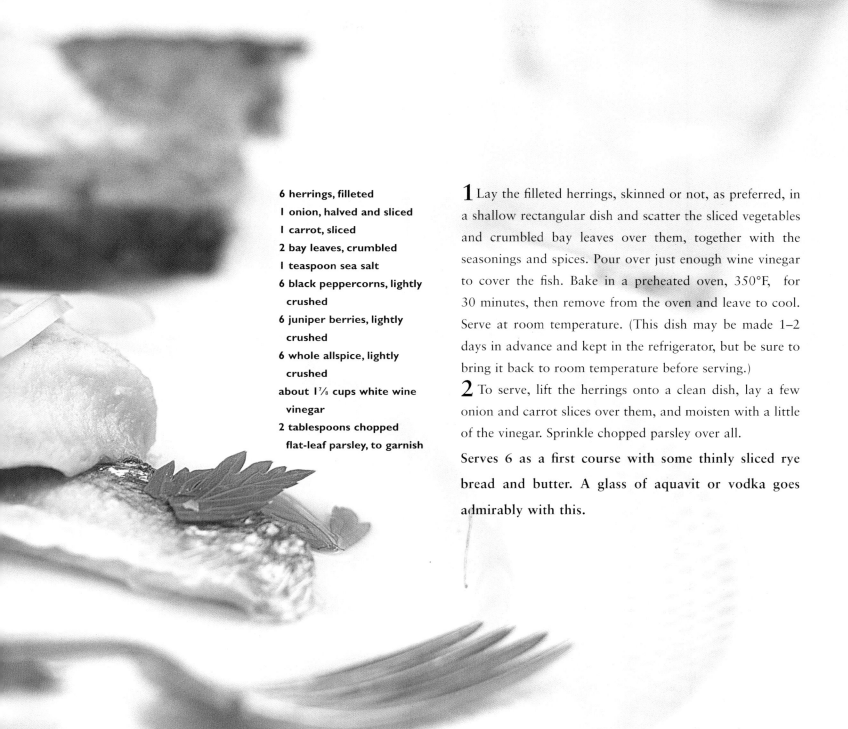

6 herrings, filleted

1 onion, halved and sliced

1 carrot, sliced

2 bay leaves, crumbled

1 teaspoon sea salt

6 black peppercorns, lightly
  crushed

6 juniper berries, lightly
  crushed

6 whole allspice, lightly
  crushed

about 1⅞ cups white wine
  vinegar

2 tablespoons chopped
  flat-leaf parsley, to garnish

1 Lay the filleted herrings, skinned or not, as preferred, in a shallow rectangular dish and scatter the sliced vegetables and crumbled bay leaves over them, together with the seasonings and spices. Pour over just enough wine vinegar to cover the fish. Bake in a preheated oven, 350°F, for 30 minutes, then remove from the oven and leave to cool. Serve at room temperature. (This dish may be made 1–2 days in advance and kept in the refrigerator, but be sure to bring it back to room temperature before serving.)

2 To serve, lift the herrings onto a clean dish, lay a few onion and carrot slices over them, and moisten with a little of the vinegar. Sprinkle chopped parsley over all.

Serves 6 as a first course with some thinly sliced rye bread and butter. A glass of aquavit or vodka goes admirably with this.

soused herrings

fish curry

This is a mild curry made in the Western way; it is not an authentic Eastern dish. It may be served at almost any temperature, except chilled.

1 Put the sliced vegetables and parsley stalks in a deep pan and cover with 4⅜ cups water. Add the ½ bay leaf, salt, and peppercorns, and bring to a boil. Simmer for 30 minutes. Then cut the fish in large pieces and add to the pan. Bring back to a boil and poach the fish for 12 minutes or until tender. Remove the fish and boil the stock until reduced and well-flavored. You will need only 2½ cups. Put the coconut in a bowl and pour 1¼ cups of the hot fish stock over it; leave for 20–30 minutes.

2 Flake the fish, removing all skin and bone, then make the sauce. Heat the butter and cook the sliced onions slowly until golden, adding the chopped garlic toward the end. Stir in the curry powder and spices, then cook for 4 minutes. Add the ground almonds and cook for another 2–3 minutes. Now pour in the remaining fish stock and simmer for 15 minutes. Strain the coconut milk, pressing lightly with the back of a wooden spoon, and add to the pan, together with the lime juice, fruit syrup or jelly, and more salt and pepper if needed. Finally, add the yogurt and do not allow it to reach boiling point. Put back the pieces of fish and reheat very gently. Just before serving, fry the sliced almonds in sunflower oil until light golden and scatter over the top. This is excellent the next day, served cold or reheated.

Serves 6 with boiled basmati rice.

I leek, sliced
I carrot, sliced
I celery stalk, sliced
3 stalks parsley
½ bay leaf
I teaspoon salt
6 black peppercorns
1½ lb. white fish: haddock, cod, or monkfish, filleted
3 tablespoons dried, flaked coconut
3 tablespoons butter
2 onions, thinly sliced
2 garlic cloves, finely chopped
I tablespoon curry powder
½ teaspoon ground turmeric
½ teaspoon ground coriander
½ teaspoon ground cumin
¼ teaspoon chili powder
½ cup ground almonds
3 tablespoons lime juice
I tablespoon fruit syrup or jelly, such as crabapple, redcurrant, blackcurrant
¼ cup yogurt
2 tablespoons sliced almonds
I tablespoon sunflower oil

spicy fish pie

1 lb. spinach
1 lb. haddock fillet
1¼ cups milk
1 bay leaf
½ tablespoon sea salt
6 black peppercorns

Spicy sauce:
2 tablespoons butter
2 tablespoons all-purpose flour
1 teaspoon Dijon mustard
1¼ cups fish stock (see recipe)
4 tablespoons light cream
1 teaspoon grated nutmeg
⅓ cup freshly grated Parmesan
  cheese
salt and black pepper

Potato purée:
1½ lb. floury potatoes
⅝ cup milk
3 tablespoons butter
sea salt and black pepper

1 Cook the spinach for 4–5 minutes in lightly salted boiling water. Drain thoroughly in a colander and leave to cool. When it is cool enough to handle, squeeze out the excess moisture, using the hands, then lay it in the bottom of a buttered soufflé dish that holds about 2½ pints.

2 Put the fish in a wide pan, pour the milk over it, and add enough water to barely cover it; then add the bay leaf, salt, and peppercorns. Bring to a boil and simmer gently for 10 minutes or until the fish is cooked through. Then lift out the fish and strain the stock; measure 1¼ cups and set aside. When the fish is cool enough to handle, discard all skin and bones, and break the fish into large flakes or chunks.

3 To make the spicy sauce, melt the butter, add the flour, and cook for 1 minute, stirring. Then stir in the mustard and the measured fish stock; bring to a boil, stirring, and simmer for 3 minutes. Then add the cream, nutmeg, freshly grated Parmesan, and salt and pepper. Mix this sauce with the flaked fish, then turn it into the soufflé dish on top of the spinach. Keep it warm.

4 Finally, make the potato purée. Boil the potatoes until tender, drain them well, then push them through a vegetable mill. Return to a clean pan and dry out over gentle heat for a few minutes while you warm the milk and butter in a small pan, adding lots of salt and black pepper. Beat the warm, buttery seasoned milk into the dry purée, then spread the purée over the fish. Bake in a preheated oven, 350°F, for 20–30 minutes.

Note: This may be made up to 1 day in advance and reheated at 325°F, for 1 hour, standing in a baking dish half full of hot water.

Serves 6

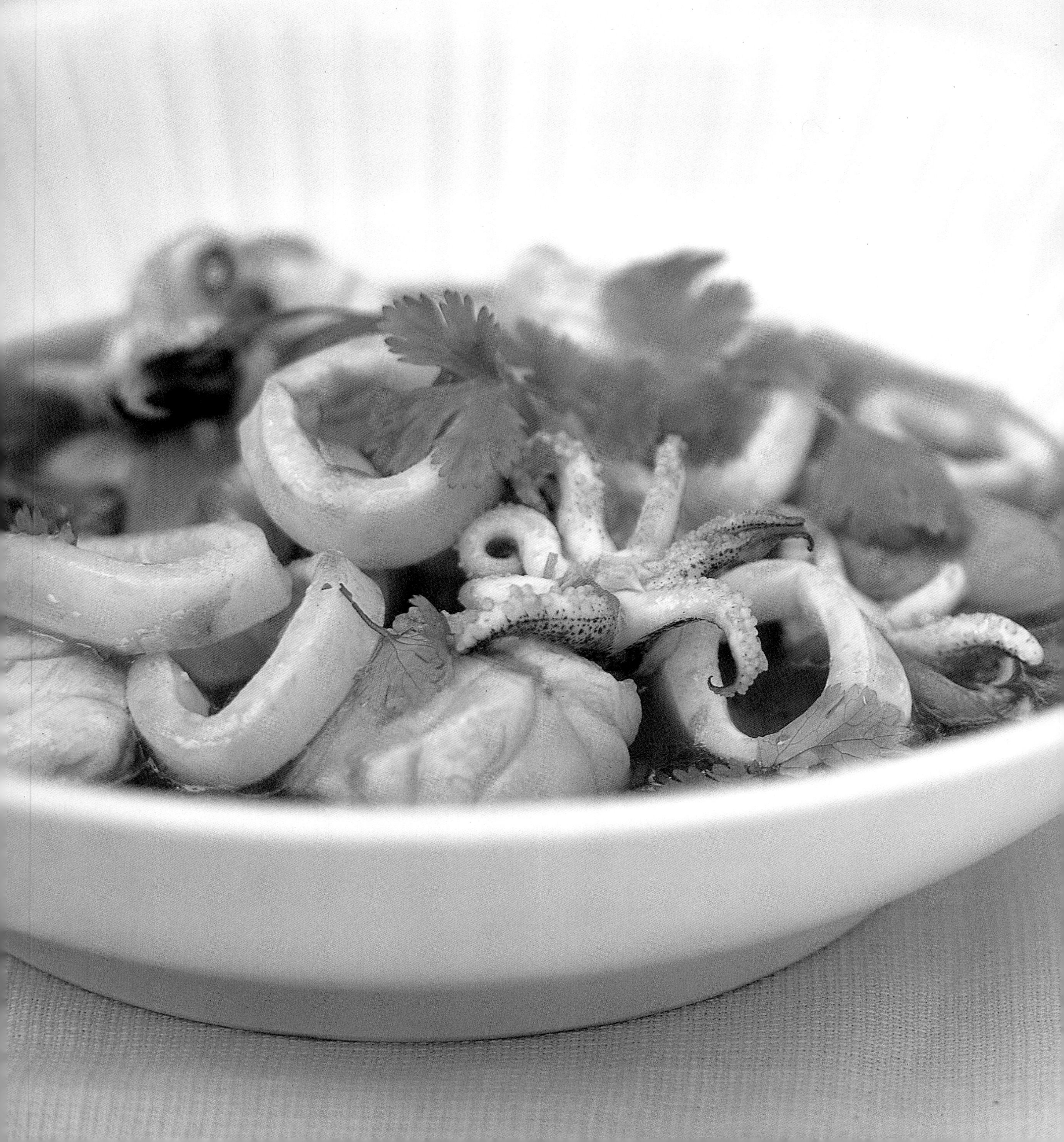

spicy seafood stew

My friend and colleague Sybil Kapoor has been kind enough to give me this recipe, which is, she says, an example of how to use one of the many varieties of dried chilies now available. Guajillo chilies have a distinctive mild, rich flavor, almost fruity, but most of the larger dried chilies may be used, except for the extra hot habañeros and Scotch bonnets. The fish and shellfish can be varied to taste.

1 Roast the chili in a preheated oven, 325°F, for 3–5 minutes or until it softens and releases a delicious aroma. (Never use burned chilies, as they are very bitter.) Remove the stalk and seeds, and soak the roasted chili for a minimum of 20 minutes in 4 tablespoons of water that has just come to a boil. Then chop the soaked chili and purée it in a small food mill with 2 tablespoons of its soaking water. Guajillo skins are very tough, so strain the purée before setting aside.

2 Meanwhile, heat the olive oil in a large saucepan and gently fry the onion and garlic until soft and golden. Add the chili purée to the onions and evaporate all the liquid before adding the tomatoes. Season with salt and black pepper; simmer gently until the tomatoes disintegrate into a mush, then stir in the lemon rind and orange juice with 3–4 tablespoons water, using just enough to thin down the mixture slightly. Simmer for another 20 minutes, adding a little more water if it seems too thick. The flavors will develop subtly if the sauce is refrigerated overnight.

3 Prepare the scallops by discarding the tough white muscle on their sides before cutting them in half. Thoroughly rinse the cleaned squid and slice into thin rings or strips. When ready to serve, bring the sauce back to a boil and add the monkfish. Simmer gently for 4 minutes before adding the scallops. Allow these to turn white (rather than opaque) and cook for 3 minutes before adding the squid and lemon juice. Allow to cook for another 4 minutes, then check the seasoning, add the cilantro leaves, and serve with rice.

Serves 4

1 dried Guajillo chili
3 tablespoons olive oil
1 onion, thinly sliced
2 garlic cloves, finely chopped
8 oz. tomatoes, skinned and
   deseeded
2 strips lemon rind, finely chopped
6 tablespoons orange juice
10 scallops, cleaned
8 oz. squid, cleaned
1 lb. monkfish fillet, cut into 1 inch
   cubes
1 tablespoon lemon juice
3 tablespoons roughly chopped
   cilantro leaves
salt and black pepper

Turkish mackerel

The combination of fish, pine nuts, currants, and allspice makes this dish unmistakably Turkish, the perfect meze.

Fry the onion in the oil until light golden brown, then add the mackerel, pine nuts, currants, ground allspice, salt, and pepper. Cook gently for 5 minutes, then stir in the chopped parsley and turn into a serving dish. Leave to cool, then sprinkle with lemon juice before serving at room temperature — do not chill.

Serves 3 to 4 as a first course, or 4 to 6 with other dishes.

1 onion, chopped
1½ tablespoons olive oil
2 mackerel, each weighing about
  8 oz., filleted, skinned, and chopped
  evenly into small pieces
2 tablespoons pine nuts
½ tablespoon currants
¼ teaspoon ground allspice
2 tablespoons chopped flat-leaf
  parsley
1½ tablespoons lemon juice
sea salt and black pepper

tiger shrimp curry

This is an adaptation of a Thai curry, made with easily accessible ingredients. Large tiger shrimps can be bought raw, usually without their heads.

1 Make the marinade first. Put the sea salt and black peppercorns in a mortar and crush briefly, just until the peppercorns are broken up. Add the crushed garlic and ginger, and pound again, until mixed. Shell the shrimps, then rinse them in cold water, pat dry, put them in the marinade and stir until well coated. Set aside to marinate for a few hours.

2 Fry the sliced onions slowly in the oil for 8–10 minutes, then add the green curry paste and cook gently for another 6–8 minutes, stirring often. Now put in the shrimps, stirring until well-mixed and pink. Next add the heated stock, salt, and black pepper, and simmer for 10 minutes. Then add the coconut milk and lime juice, and cook for another 1–2 minutes. Turn into a serving dish and scatter the chopped cilantro over the top. Accompany with a dish of basmati rice.

Serves 4

8 oz. onions, thinly sliced
4 tablespoons sunflower oil
2 tablespoons Green Curry Paste
  (see page 214)
1 lb. raw tiger shrimps, without heads
1¼ cups chicken stock, heated
⅝ cup Coconut Milk (see page 215)
3 tablespoons lime juice
salt and black pepper
3 tablespoons cilantro leaves, coarsely
  chopped, to garnish

Marinade:
1 teaspoon sea salt
20 black peppercorns
2 large garlic cloves, crushed in press
2 oz. fresh root ginger, peeled and
  crushed in press

marinated hake
in coconut milk

When hake is not available, use cod or gray mullet for this excellent Fijian dish.

1 Put the pieces of fish in a bowl and add the lemon juice. There should be enough to come almost level with the fish. Leave for 15 minutes to marinate, turning the fish over from time to time so that all surfaces come in contact with the lemon juice.

2 When the time is up, add the salt, then stir in the chopped onion, scallions, chili, and cucumber. Then pour on the coconut milk, stirring gently until blended with the lemon juice, and add the torn cilantro leaves. This is best served soon after making, in shallow bowls at room temperature; but it may be kept in the refrigerator for 1–2 hours as long as it is taken out 30 minutes before serving.

Serves 4 as a first course.

- **1½ lb. hake, skinned, boned, and cut in ½ inch squares**
- **6 tablespoons lemon juice**
- **1 teaspoon sea salt**
- **½ onion, finely chopped**
- **2 scallions, sliced ¼ inch thick**
- **1 small red chili, deseeded and finely chopped**
- **¼ cucumber, peeled and cut in small pieces**
- **⅝ cup Coconut Milk (see page 215)**
- **2 tablespoons cilantro leaves, torn**

shrimp cakes with cilantro

1 Put the shelled shrimps in a food processor with the scallions, ginger, ground coriander, cilantro, soft breadcrumbs, salt, and pepper. Process until thoroughly blended. Then beat 1 egg and add it and the lemon juice, and process again briefly. Put the shrimp mixture into a bowl and chill in the refrigerator for about 1 hour.

2 Beat the remaining egg. Form the chilled mixture into large round cakes, dip them in a little flour, then in the beaten egg, then the dry breadcrumbs. Heat a little sunflower oil, just enough to make a layer ¼ inch deep, in a skillet, then put in the shrimp cakes and fry them for about 8 minutes on each side, until nicely browned and cooked through; remembering that, unlike most fish cakes, these are made from raw fish and need more than surface cooking. Garnish with lemon quarters.

Makes 6 shrimp cakes; serves 6 as a first course with a little salad, or 3 as a main dish.

- **1 lb. large raw shrimps, without heads, (about 2¼ cups after shelling)**
- **1 bunch scallions, sliced**
- **1½ tablespoons finely chopped fresh root ginger**
- **½ tablespoon ground coriander**
- **2 tablespoons chopped cilantro**
- **3 tablespoons soft white breadcrumbs**
- **½ tablespoon sea salt**
- **2 eggs**
- **3 tablespoons lemon juice**
- **a little all-purpose flour**
- **dry white breadcrumbs**
- **sunflower oil, for shallow frying**
- **black pepper**
- **2 lemons, cut in quarters, to garnish**

Best for broiling are the large freshwater king shrimps, sold raw, in the shell, but with the heads removed. Also good are tiger shrimps, as long as they, too, are raw.

1 Put the oil in a small pan with the hot red pepper flakes. Warm gently over low heat for 4 minutes, then leave to cool.

2 When ready to cook, heat the broiler and thread the shrimps on skewers, leaving the shells on. Allow 4–5 shrimps for each person. Brush the shrimps on both sides with the chili oil and broil for 3 minutes on each side. They may be served still on the skewers, or slid off onto a mound of buttered rice mixed with chopped herbs. Serve with quartered lemons and a bowl of mayonnaise.

Note: For a tidy dish, you may shell the shrimps before broiling. In this case broil for 2 minutes on each side.

Serves 4 as a main dish with a green salad.

3 tablespoons virgin olive oil
½ teaspoon hot red pepper flakes
16–20 large raw shrimps
2 lemons, cut in quarters, to garnish

broiled shrimps
with chili oil

stir-fried squid
with ginger and chilies

1 To prepare the squid, pull the head and its attachments out of the body sac. Cut across the head between the tentacles and the eyes; reserve the tentacles and discard the rest. Squeeze out the small polyp in the center of the tentacles and discard. Wash the body sac under cold running water, pulling out the inner quill and discarding it, along with any other odds and ends inside the sac. Pull away the outer skin; cut off the triangular side fins and reserve. Cut the body sac across in rings about ¼ inch wide. Leave the tentacles in clumps.

2 Heat a wok or deep round pan. Add the oil and heat again, then throw in the prepared squid rings, tentacles, and fins, and toss for 2–3 minutes, adding the scallions, chili, and ginger halfway through. When the time is up, add the sugar, salt and *sake* or vermouth. Toss for 1 minute. Serve immediately, with rice.

Serves 3 to 4

1 lb. small squid

3 tablespoons sunflower oil

6 scallions, sliced

1 green chili, deseeded and finely chopped

2 teaspoons finely chopped fresh root ginger

1 teaspoon sugar

½ teaspoon sea salt

1 tablespoon *sake* or dry vermouth

stir-fried shrimps

This is especially good when made with Seville oranges.

Heat a wok or deep sauté pan. Add the oil and heat again, then throw in the sliced scallions and toss for 30 seconds. Add the chilies and ginger and toss for another 30 seconds; then add the shrimps and stir-fry for 2 minutes. Add the fruit juice and soy sauce and continue to stir-fry for another minute. Remove from the heat and stir in the chopped cilantro.

Note: You can use 1 lb. scallops instead of shrimps. Discard the orange tongues and cut the scallops in halves or quarters, depending on the size.

Serves 2 to 3 with boiled rice.

2 tablespoons sunflower oil

1 bunch scallions, sliced

2 green chilies, deseeded and finely chopped

1½ tablespoons finely chopped fresh root ginger

2¼ cups shelled shrimps

3 tablespoons Seville orange juice or 2 tablespoons sweet orange juice and 1 tablespoon lemon juice

1 tablespoon soy sauce

3 tablespoons chopped cilantro

pickled swordfish

In Turkey this is made with swordfish, but any firm-fleshed fish, such as tuna or halibut, may be used instead.

1 Prepare 3 days in advance. Wash and dry the fish steaks, then sprinkle them with sea salt. Heat the oil in a wide skillet and cook the steaks quickly until lightly browned on each side, without being cooked through. Remove them and leave to cool.

2 Soak the saffron in 3 tablespoons hot water for 10 minutes, then put the saffron water in a pan with the vinegar and sugar. Bring to a boil, stirring, and cook for 3 minutes, or until the sugar has melted.

3 Put half the bay leaves in the bottom of a wide dish and lay half the fish steaks on them. Sprinkle with half the garlic, allspice, peppercorns, and pistachios. Add the remaining fish, bay leaves, and spices. Pour the saffron vinegar on top; there should be just enough to cover the fish. Press down lightly with a small plate and a 1 lb. weight. Cover and keep in the refrigerator for 3 days before eating. (It may be kept up to 6 days, but after this the flavor will deteriorate.) Transfer to a flat dish to serve, dividing the steaks into smaller pieces. Sprinkle with flat-leaf parsley, to garnish.

Serves 4 to 6 as a first course, or more with other dishes.

4–6 swordfish steaks about ¾ inch thick
2 tablespoons olive oil
¼ teaspoon saffron threads
2½ cups white wine vinegar
1 tablespoon sugar
6 bay leaves
4 garlic cloves, coarsely chopped
½ teaspoon whole allspice
2 teaspoons black peppercorns
¼ cup shelled pistachios, halved
sea salt
1½ tablespoons chopped flat-leaf parsley, to garnish

To add interest to broiled chicken, serve accompanied by a small bowl of ground paprika that has been fried in a little light olive oil. Add in minute amounts. This is also delicious drizzled over dishes of hummus, sliced cheese, and goulash.

poultry and game

Caribbean fried chicken

This may be made with a whole chicken, cut up, or with pieces sold in packs in the supermarket. I find it works best with boned pieces, not too thick. Best of all are the filleted chicken breasts, which cook very quickly. Also good are thighs, boned and cut in half.

1 Some hours in advance, or the night before, make small slits in the skin side of the chicken. Rub all over with the West Indian seasoning, pressing it well into the cuts. Set aside, or in the refrigerator if for longer than 2 hours, until ready to cook.
2 To make the batter, mix the egg, flour, and milk in a food processor or by hand. Heat a 1 inch layer of oil in a heavy skillet. Just before frying, process or beat the batter again; dip each chicken piece in batter, then in the breadcrumbs. When the oil is very hot, put in half the chicken and cook for 4–8 minutes on each side. Halved chicken breasts take 4 minutes on each side, whole ones 6–7 minutes; halved thighs 5–6 minutes. Serve hot as soon as possible after cooking.
Note: This is excellent picnic food, good at any temperature and easy to eat.

Serves 4 with rice and a green salad.

3½ lb. chicken, cut up, or
  1½–2 lb. chicken pieces
West Indian Seasoning (see page 223)
dry white breadcrumbs
sunflower oil, for frying

Batter:
1 egg, beaten
¾ cup all-purpose flour, sifted
⅝ cup milk

broiled chicken
in saffron marinade

1 Make small cuts in the top surface of the meat. Soak the chilies for 10 minutes in 4 tablespoons boiling water, then drain the chilies and chop them, reserving the water. Put the chopped chilies in a small mill with half their soaking water and process to a purée. Mix with the ginger, garlic, salt, and spices. Stir this into the yogurt, mixing well. Lastly, stir in the oil and lemon juice. Pour some of the marinade over the meat, making sure it is well covered. Leave for several hours or overnight in the refrigerator, turning once or twice and adding more of marinade.
2 Shortly before serving, line the broiler pan with foil and lay the chicken pieces on it — do not use the rack. Spoon some of the marinade over the chicken pieces and broil them for 5 minutes on each side, turning once. Add a fresh layer of marinade before broiling the second side. Serve as soon as possible after cooking.

Serves 4 as a light main dish with boiled rice and a green salad.

1½ lb. chicken breasts cut into 2–3
  pieces each

Marinade:
3 dried chilies, deseeded and chopped
1 tablespoon grated fresh root ginger
3 garlic cloves, crushed
1 teaspoon salt
1 teaspoon ground cumin
½ teaspoon ground coriander
¼ teaspoon powdered saffron
1¼ cups thick yogurt
3 tablespoons sunflower oil
⅝ cup lemon juice

COUSCOUS with chicken wings

12 chicken wings

1⅓–1⅔ cups couscous

2 tablespoons light olive oil or sunflower oil

4–6 pickling onions, peeled

3–4 small leeks, cut in 1 inch chunks

3–4 small carrots, cut in 1 inch chunks

½ teaspoon saffron threads

3 small tomatoes, cut in halves or quarters

Hot Sauce I or II (see page 185) (optional)

1 tablespoon cilantro leaves, torn in pieces, to garnish

Spice mixture:

1 teaspoon ground cumin

½ teaspoon ground coriander

½ teaspoon chili powder

1 tablespoon tomato purée

salt and black pepper

1 Make the spice mixture first: mix the spices with salt and pepper and stir into the tomato purée. Rub this paste all over the chicken wings and leave for 1–2 hours.

2 Put the couscous in a bowl and pour 1–1¼ cups cold water over it. Leave for 10 minutes, then pour into the top part of a *couscousier* or a strainer lined with cheesecloth. Heat the oil in a heavy pan and brown the chicken wings quickly. Then transfer them to a pan into which the strainer fits nicely, leaving plenty of room for the simmering liquid below. Add enough hot water to cover the wings generously, and bring to a boil. Now add the onions, leeks, and carrots, and bring back to a boil. Place the strainer over the pot, cover with a lid, and cook steadily for 30 minutes. Pound the saffron in a mortar, add 2 tablespoons of the hot stock and leave for 10 minutes, then add to the rest of the simmering stock. Then add the tomatoes to the pot, replace the couscous and cook for another 12–15 minutes. Towards the end of the time make the hot sauce, taking a little of the simmering chicken stew to mix with it.

3 To serve, pour the couscous onto a dish, breaking up any lumps and moistening it with a little of the chicken stew. Using a slotted spoon, lift out a few of the vegetables and lay them over the couscous, then scatter the cilantro leaves over all. Put the chicken wings on a separate dish and pour the rest of the vegetables and the stew into a tureen or deep bowl. Serve in soup plates, with knife, fork, and spoon, and the hot sauce in a small dish.

Note: If you don't want to make the hot sauce, simply serve a good bottled variety, such as Tabasco or any of the new hot sauces, on the table.

Serves 6

Neither tamarind nor curry leaves are essential for this dish, but coconut milk definitely is.

I lb. boneless chicken, cut in
   strips or cubes

8 oz. onions, sliced

4 tablespoons sunflower oil

2 tablespoons Green Curry
   Paste (see page 214)

1⅛ cups chicken stock,
   heated

1¼ cups Coconut Milk (see
   page 215)

3 tablespoons tamarind
   water (see page 50) or
   semi-acidic fruit juice, such
   as Seville orange, pink
   grapefruit, or lime

15 fresh curry leaves, to
   garnish (optional)

salt and black pepper

Marinade:

I teaspoon sea salt

20 black peppercorns

2 large garlic cloves, crushed
   in press

2 oz. fresh root ginger, peeled
   and crushed in press

1 To make the marinade, put the sea salt and black peppercorns in a mortar and pound briefly. Add the crushed garlic and ginger and pound again, just until mixed. Turn the chicken pieces in the marinade and mix well. Set aside for a few hours or overnight.

2 Cook the sliced onions slowly in the oil, allowing about 12 minutes for them to soften and color. Then add the curry paste and cook gently for 8 minutes, stirring often. Now add the chicken pieces, stirring until they have browned all over. Add the heated stock, salt, and black pepper, and simmer for 20 minutes. Then add the coconut milk and tamarind water or fruit juice, and cook for another 3 minutes, adding the curry leaves, if using. Turn into a dish to serve, with basmati rice.

Serves 4

green curried chicken

chicken croquettes
with salsa

1 Start 1 day in advance. Put the chicken in a deep pan and add the flavoring vegetables and herbs, measured salt, and peppercorns. Add enough hot water to cover the thighs and bring quickly to a boil. Skim once or twice, then poach gently for 1¼ hours or until the meat is tender. Leave to cool in the stock, if time permits, then lift out and drain well. Discard all skin and bone, and dice the meat. You need 1 lb. of diced chicken. Strain the stock and reserve for another dish.

2 Melt the butter in a pan, stir in the flour and cook for 1 minute. Then add the heated milk and simmer for 3 minutes, stirring often. Stir in the chopped chicken, garam masala or mace, chopped parsley, salt, and pepper. Spread the mixture in a shallow dish and leave to cool, then chill in the refrigerator for a few hours, until firm.

3 Form the mixture into cork-shaped croquettes and dip them in the beaten egg and then the dry white breadcrumbs. Heat the butter and oil in a wide skillet. When it is very hot, put in some of the croquettes in one layer, and fry them until golden brown all over. Drain them on paper towels while you fry the next batch. Serve as soon as possible, with the salsa.

Makes 16 to 18 croquettes; serves 6.

3½ lb. roasting chicken
I onion, halved
I leek, halved
I carrot, halved
I celery stalk, halved
I bay leaf
½ tablespoon salt
8 black peppercorns
3 tablespoons butter
¼ cup all-purpose flour
I cup milk, heated
I teaspoon garam masala or mace
1½ tablespoons finely chopped
  parsley
I egg, beaten
dry white breadcrumbs
2 tablespoons butter
2 tablespoons sunflower oil
salt and black pepper
Salsa Fresca (see page 191) or
  Smoky Salsa (see page 187),
  to serve

Suna's colonial chicken curry

This is an Anglicized version of a curry, not for purists, but quite delicious all the same. Basically mild in character, it is good served with one or two spicy relishes. It is best made a day in advance.

3½ lb. chicken

flavoring vegetables: onion, leek,
  carrot, celery, bay leaf

½ tablespoon sea salt

8 black peppercorns

2 onions, chopped

2½ tablespoons sunflower oil

2 garlic cloves, chopped

2 carrots, chopped

1 green pepper, chopped

1 red pepper, chopped

1½ tablespoons light curry powder

4½ tablespoons all-purpose flour

2½ cups chicken stock (see recipe)

2 tablespoons sultanas or white
  raisins

1 Granny Smith apple, quartered,
  cored and chopped

1 tablespoon chopped fresh root
  ginger

1 teaspoon turmeric

1 tablespoon mango chutney, chopped

13 oz. tomatoes, skinned and
  coarsely chopped

2 tablespoons lemon juice

1–2 teaspoons garam masala
  (optional)

2 tablespoons butter

1⅞ cups milk, heated

⅝ cup light cream

salt and black pepper

2 tablespoons chopped cilantro
  leaves, to garnish

1 Start 1 day in advance, if possible, as the curry improves on keeping. Put the chicken in a pressure cooker with the flavoring vegetables, measured salt, and peppercorns. Pour on enough hot water to cover the thighs of the chicken, screw down the lid, and bring to a boil. Cook under pressure for 25 minutes, then reduce the pressure and take out the chicken. Alternatively, cook the chicken in an ordinary pan for 1¼ hours. Take the meat off the bones and return the carcass to the pressure cooker or pan. Bring back to a boil and cook for another 25 minutes under pressure or 1¼ hours in an ordinary pan. Then strain the stock and set aside to cool.

2 Fry the onions slowly in the sunflower oil, adding the garlic after 5 minutes. After another 5 minutes add the chopped carrots and peppers. Fry gently for 2–3 minutes, stirring, then add the curry powder and 2½ tablespoons of the flour, and cook for 1 minute. Then remove the fat from the chicken stock and measure 2½ cups of stock. Add it to the vegetables and stir until blended. Simmer gently for 5 minutes, then add the sultanas, apple, ginger, turmeric, and chutney. Continue to simmer gently for 30 minutes, then add the tomatoes and cook for another 15 minutes. When the time is up, add the lemon juice, and a little garam masala if you wish to increase the heat; remove from the stove. Allow to cool for 10–15 minutes, then purée briefly in a food processor; it should not be too smooth.

3 In a clean pan, melt the butter, stir in the remaining flour, and cook for 1 minute. Then add the heated milk and stir until it reaches boiling point. Simmer gently for 5 minutes, add the cream, then mix well with the curried vegetable sauce. Add the chicken pieces and reheat gently before serving, sprinkled with the chopped cilantro leaves.

Serves 6 to 8 with saffron-flavored rice, or basmati rice, and one or two of the following relishes: Salsa Fresca (see page 191), Cucumber Raita (see page 218), or Mango Relish (see page 220).

spiced chicken salad

Here is a useful dish to serve after Chicken Broth with Ginger Dumplings (see page 73), since a large poached chicken will provide enough white meat for the salad at the same time as a well-flavored stock for the soup. This pair of dishes deserves an organically reared, or at least free-range, chicken for optimum flavor and texture.

4 lb. roasting chicken

I onion cut in 4

I leek, cut in 4

I large carrot, cut in 4

I celery stalk, halved

I bay leaf

½ tablespoon sea salt

10 black peppercorns

Salad:

6 sun-dried tomato pieces, rinsed

4 oz. arugula or young spinach
   leaves, washed and drained

¼ cucumber, peeled, cut in 4 lengthwise and sliced

I red chili, deseeded and cut in thin
   rings

Dressing:

5 tablespoons extra virgin olive oil

2 tablespoons lemon juice

½ tablespoon white wine vinegar

5–6 drops chili oil

1 Begin 1 day in advance. Put the chicken in a deep pot or pressure cooker with the flavoring vegetables, bay leaf, and seasonings. Add enough water to just cover the legs, leaving most of the breast uncovered. Bring to a boil, cover the pan and simmer for 1 hour 20 minutes, or 17 minutes under pressure, until the breast meat is cooked — the legs do not matter. Turn off the heat and leave to cool overnight.

2 Next day take out the chicken and cut off the breast fillets in 2 large pieces, with the skin attached. Wrap them in plastic wrap until shortly before serving so that they don't dry out. Put the rest of the chicken back in the stock and boil again for 1½ hours, or 30 minutes under pressure, to make a truly delicious consommé.

3 Before assembling the salad, cover the sun-dried tomatoes with boiling water and let stand for 5 minutes; then drain them, pat dry, and cut in broad strips. Divide the chicken breast into neat fillets, using a knife and fingers. Pile the salad leaves in a large dish and scatter the sliced cucumber, dried tomatoes, and chili rings over all. Mix the dressing ingredients together and pour most of the dressing over the salad. Toss well, then lay the chicken fillets over the top and moisten them with the rest of the dressing. Serve immediately with toasted pita bread.

Serves 4 as a light main dish.

Chinese duck pancakes

It would be presumptuous to call this Peking duck, since it is only a very modest approximation of the real thing, but it is good nonetheless and fun to eat. It must be eaten with your fingers and makes a perfect meal for 2–4 people. A whole duck will feed 4, while half a duck will feed 2 admirably.

1 Make the pancake batter a few hours in advance. Put the flours, unsifted, into a food processor with the salt. While processing, pour the beaten eggs through the lid, then the sunflower oil, and the mixed milk and water, stopping when you have a mixture like fairly thick cream. Leave for 1–2 hours.

2 Prick the duck all over with a skewer, then rub with sea salt. Lay it upside down in a roasting pan. Roast in a preheated oven, 400°F, for 1 hour. Turn it right side up and roast for another 40 minutes; it needs to be well done.

3 While the duck is roasting, prepare the scallions. Take 3 of the fattest ones and make several cuts upward in the white end about 1 inch deep and ¼ inch apart, then splay them outwards to form a brush. (Sumatra-born Sri Owen describes how to do this with lemon grass in *Indonesian Regional Food and Cookery* and has kindly allowed me to adapt her idea.) Place the hot chili sauce in a bowl with the scallion brushes laid in it. Cut the rest of the scallions into thin slivers about 4 inches long and lay them in a dish.

4 To make the pancakes, process the batter again, heat a small skillet and grease it with a tiny piece of butter. Pour in 2 tablespoons of batter, and spread evenly. Cook for 1 minute on each side; transfer to a warm dish while you repeat the process.

5 To serve, use 2 forks to pull the duck meat off the bone and into shreds. Serve the hot pancakes, hot duck, and cold scallions on separate dishes. Use the scallions to dab the chili sauce onto the pancake filling before rolling it up.

6 For serving 2, ask your butcher to cut a duck in half. Wrap half in foil and freeze. Place the remaining duck upside down on a rack in a roasting pan and roast in a preheated oven, 400°F, covered loosely with foil, for 30 minutes, then remove the foil, turn the duck over and cook for 35 minutes. Make the whole pancake batter recipe. Fry all the pancakes, wrap half in foil, interleaving with squares of waxed paper, and freeze. To reheat, thaw to room temperature, loosen the foil and lay them in the top of a steamer for 5 minutes.

Makes about 18 pancakes measuring 5½ inches wide; serves 4.

Hot Chili Sauce (see page 182), made in advance, to serve

Pancakes:
¾ cup whole wheat flour
¾ cup white bread flour or all-purpose flour
½ teaspoon sea salt
2 eggs, beaten
1 tablespoon sunflower oil
⅝ cup milk mixed with ⅝ cup water
butter

Filling:
1 duck
2 bunches scallions
sea salt

deviled chicken wings

This is an old-fashioned English dish, much used for reheating pieces of roast chicken or pheasant. Chicken drumsticks can be substituted for wings; indeed, any pieces can be treated in this way; the wings are particularly good, especially as a light meal or snack.

1 Remove the extreme end (third joint) of the wings. To make the sauce, mix the two mustards with the chopped chutney and Worcestershire sauce. Make small slits in the chicken pieces, using a small sharp knife and cutting through the skin about ½ inch deep. Rub the devil sauce all over the meat, pressing it well into the cuts. Leave for 1–2 hours before cooking. Then heat the broiler and coat the chicken pieces in breadcrumbs. Line the broiler pan with foil and lay the chicken pieces on it. Don't use the rack, as this will rub off the coating. Dot the wings with butter and broil for 4–5 minutes on each side, until well browned. These may be served immediately, or later, while still warm, or after cooling.

2 Drumsticks or other pieces may be treated in the same way; adjust the timing accordingly. Drumsticks will take approximately 8–9 minutes on each side.

Serves 3 to 4 as a light meal or snack.

1½ lb. chicken wings
dry white breadcrumbs
1 tablespoon butter

Devil sauce:
1 tablespoon Dijon mustard
1 tablespoon prepared English mustard
4 tablespoons chutney, chopped (preferably not mango, which is too sweet)
1½ tablespoons Worcestershire sauce

stir-fried chicken
with red pepper flakes

1 Put the chicken strips in a bowl. Pour the soy sauce over them, adding the sugar, if using. Crush the ginger in a garlic press and add the juice to the chicken strips; discard the debris left in the press. Let the chicken stand for 30 minutes.

2 When the time is up, heat a wok. Add enough oil to cover the bottom and heat again, then throw in the sliced onion and garlic. Cook for 3–4 minutes, stirring, then add the chicken and its marinade, and the red pepper flakes. Stir for 4 minutes more, until the chicken is cooked through. Add the bean sprouts and cook for 1 minute longer. Turn onto a dish and scatter with the chopped cilantro.

Note: Rump steak or pork fillet may be substituted for the chicken.

Serves 4 with rice.

2 chicken breasts, boned and cut into thin strips
4 tablespoons soy sauce
½ teaspoon sugar (optional)
2 inch square fresh root ginger, peeled and cut in ½ inch chunks
3–4 tablespoons sunflower oil
2 onions, sliced
3 garlic cloves, sliced
½ teaspoon hot red pepper flakes
3 cups bean sprouts, rinsed
3 tablespoons chopped cilantro leaves, to garnish

braised pheasants
with lemon grass

1 If serving cold, start 1 day in advance, and first braise the celeriac, omitting the cumin and coriander and reserving the stock. Heat the oil in a casserole and brown the birds all over. Sprinkle them with sea salt and black pepper. Lay them on their sides and tuck the lemon grass, garlic, ginger, juniper berries, and peppercorns all around them. Pour the heated stock over them (if serving cold, the celeriac stock may be substituted for the same amount of chicken stock) and bring to the boiling point. Cover the casserole and cook in a preheated oven, 375°F, for 30 minutes. When the time is up, remove the hen but leave the cock in the oven for another 5 minutes. If eating cold, leave both birds to cool in the pan, then remove them and strain the stock.

2 Next day skim off the fat and carve the birds in thin slices, cutting the larger slices in half. Carve the wings and legs into 6 neat joints for each bird. Lay the spinach on a flat dish. Mix the oil and lemon juice with 2 tablespoons of the strained stock, then add the soy sauce or balsamic vinegar, and mix again. Pour half of this over the spinach, then intersperse slices of apple among the braised celeriac, spreading them over the bed of spinach. Lay the pheasant slices over this, reserving the joints, and spoon the rest of the sauce over all. Sprinkle with chopped chervil and serve. The joints may be served on a separate dish or kept for another meal.

Serves 8 as a first course, or 6 as a light main dish.

For a hot dish, allow an extra 5 minutes roasting for each bird, then carve as above, laying joints and slices over a dish of freshly cooked noodles. Mix the strained and degreased pan juices with the soy sauce or balsamic vinegar, then pour over all.

Serves 6 to 8 as a main dish with a green salad.

1½ lb. celeriac, braised (see page 150)
3 tablespoons sunflower oil
1 brace pheasants (1 cock, 1 hen)
6 stalks lemon grass
6 garlic cloves, unpeeled and coarsely crushed
1 oz. fresh root ginger, cut in 4 and coarsely crushed
6 juniper berries, coarsely crushed
6 black peppercorns, coarsely crushed
1¼ cups chicken stock, heated
sea salt and black pepper

Garnish for a cold dish:
4 oz. spinach
2 tablespoons extra virgin olive oil
2 tablespoons lemon juice
1 tablespoon soy sauce or balsamic vinegar
1 hard, green apple, peeled, quartered, and thickly sliced
1½ tablespoons chopped chervil

Garnish for a hot dish:
8 oz. egg noodles, freshly boiled and drained
1 tablespoon soy sauce or balsamic vinegar

For a simple supper dish sprinkle Za'atar (see page 62) over pan-fried lamb cutlets or noisettes of lamb.

meat

roast lamb with coriander

This dish is best made with coriander seeds that have been roughly crushed. This can be done in a mortar or using a rolling pin; an electric mill gives too fine a texture.

1 Make small cuts about 1 inch long and 1 inch deep in the fat on the top surface of the leg. Push the crushed coriander seeds into the cuts. If using garlic, push thin slivers into the cuts beside the coriander. Lay the leg on a rack in a roasting pan and roast in a preheated oven, 350°F, for 30 minutes per 1 lb.

2 Halfway through the cooking, remove the pan from the oven and pour off the fat. Pour the heated red wine over the meat. Baste once or twice during the rest of the cooking. When the meat is done, remove it from the oven and lay it on a carving dish. Cover it with a large piece of foil and a thick towel, and let rest for 20–30 minutes before carving. Pour the juices from the pan into a sauceboat; keep warm.

Serves 6 to 8

I leg of lamb
3 tablespoons whole coriander seeds, coarsely crushed
2 garlic cloves, peeled and cut in slivers (optional)
I cup red wine, heated

red curried beef

1 Start 1 day in advance. Heat 3 tablespoons of the oil in a heavy pan and brown the cubed beef. Transfer it to a dish while you first fry the onion, then the potatoes, adding another 2 tablespoons oil for each. Allow about 8 minutes each for them to become light golden, then add them to the beef. Fry the curry paste gently for 2 minutes in the same pan, adding the tamarind syrup, or the tamarind purée, and brown sugar dissolved in 3 tablespoons hot water. Add the coconut milk and mix well, then bring to a boil and replace the beef and vegetables. Bring back to a boil, adding salt and black pepper. Cook gently, covered, for 2–3 hours, until the beef is tender. Leave to cool overnight.

2 Next day remove the fat from the surface of the dish. Add salt and pepper and the lime juice. Serve with plain rice and Apple Relish made without chili powder (see page 218), or Cucumber Raita (see page 218), or Mango Relish (see page 220).

Serves 4 to 6

½ cup vegetable oil
1½ lb. stewing beef, cut in
 I inch cubes
12 oz. onions, halved and thickly sliced
12 oz. potatoes, peeled and thickly sliced
2 tablespoons Red Curry Paste (see page 214)
4 tablespoons Tamarind Syrup (see page 222), or I tablespoon tamarind purée and ½ tablespoon brown sugar
2¼ cups Coconut Milk (see page 215)
2–3 tablespoons lime juice
salt and black pepper

poached beef in spiced broth

If you cannot get wasabi or fresh horseradish — don't even dream of using bottled horseradish — for the sauce, you can use grated ginger instead.

3¾ cups good beef or chicken stock
   (see page 71 or 73)
2 stalks lemon grass, peeled and
   roughly crushed
2 whole chilies, red or green
6 sirloin steaks, cut about ¼ inch
   thick and weighing about
   3 oz. each
4 scallions, cut in 1 inch lengths, to
   garnish

Sauce:
3 tablespoons *sake* or dry vermouth
3 tablespoons light soy sauce
2 teaspoons wasabi (see page 53) or
   grated fresh horseradish, or 1 oz.
   fresh root ginger, peeled and grated

1 Heat the stock in a wide pan, adding the lemon grass and chilies. Bring it slowly to a boil, then simmer very gently, half covered, while you cut the fat off the steaks and make the sauce.

2 Mix the sauce ingredients in a pitcher. Prepare the garnish by cutting the scallion sections into thin slivers. Shortly before serving, when the stock has been gently simmering for 15–20 minutes, lower the steaks into the stock 2 at a time and poach for exactly 1 minute. Then lift them out and keep them warm while you cook the rest. When all are cooked, discard the lemon grass and chilies, and mix 3 tablespoons of the hot stock into the sauce and pour a little of it over the steaks. Scatter the scallions over the beef and serve immediately, with the rest of the sauce in a pitcher.

Serves 6 with noodles and a green vegetable.

tripe with chilies

2 tablespoons sunflower oil
1 onion, sliced
2 garlic cloves, sliced
1 red chili, with seeds, sliced
13 oz. canned tomatoes
6 marjoram leaves
salt
1 lb. precooked tripe, cut in
   1 inch squares
freshly grated Parmesan cheese,
   to serve

Now that tripe can be bought precooked, it has become an eminently sensible buy. In this recipe the bland quality of the tripe is offset by the sharp bite of fresh chilies.

Heat the oil in a pan and fry the onion, garlic, and chili. Cook briskly, until slightly brown; add the canned tomatoes, chopping them roughly in the pan with the edge of a wooden spoon. Add the marjoram and salt, cover the pan and cook gently for about 10 minutes. Then add the tripe, stirring; cover and cook for 15 minutes. This is best served in bowls and eaten with spoons. Serve with Parmesan.

Serves 4 as a one-course meal.

coriander steak

This recipe is an aromatic version of steak au poivre, based on whole coriander seeds instead of peppercorns.

2 tablespoons whole coriander seeds

1 tablespoon black mustard seeds

2 teaspoons black peppercorns

2 teaspoons sea salt

4 sirloin steaks

2 tablespoons butter

1½ tablespoons sunflower oil

Put the coriander seeds in a mortar with the mustard seeds, peppercorns, and sea salt. Crush them roughly, then use to coat the steaks on both sides. Leave for 1 hour or longer. Then heat the butter and oil in a heavy skillet. When the fat is very hot, put in the steaks and fry briefly on each side, trying not to knock off more of the spices than you can help. Serve with a Fresh Tomato Sauce (see page 185), or a Smoky Salsa (see page 187), served at room temperature.

Serves 4

spiced beef

This is an old English dish that has been popular since Elizabethan times or earlier. Saltpeter is no longer obtainable, but the salt and spices combine to preserve the beef satisfactorily. You need to begin 15 days before you want to serve the beef.

1 Mix the sugar with all the spices except the salt and rub the mixture into the beef. Lay it in an earthenware crock, cover with a lid and leave it for 3 days. Then add half the salt, rubbing it in well with the spices. Return the beef to the crock and leave for another 4 days, turning it over in the spices every day. (A brine will soon form as the salt brings out the juices in the meat.) Then add half the remaining salt, and the remainder 4 days later. After the beef has been in the crock for 2 weeks it will be ready to cook.

2 Rinse off all the salt and spices and put the beef in a casserole with 1¼ cups water. Cover with 2 sheets of foil and the lid, and cook in the bottom of a preheated oven, 275°F, for 45–50 minutes per 1 lb. — the timing will depend on the shape of the meat. When the time is up, take the meat out of the oven and leave to cool for 2–3 hours in the casserole. Then lift the meat out, lay it on a flat surface and weigh it down with a board. Set 3 weights of 2 lb. each on the board and leave overnight. Next day wrap the beef in foil and place it in the refrigerator, taking it out 1–2 hours before serving. It should keep for 12–14 days under refrigeration. To serve, cut the beef in thin slices and accompany with a fruit pickle, baked potatoes, and a green salad — perfect summer vacation fare.

Serves 4 to 6 for 2 to 3 meals.

⅓ **cup dark muscovado sugar**

1 **teaspoon ground mace**

1 **teaspoon coarsely ground black pepper**

2 **tablespoons juniper berries, coarsely crushed**

2 **teaspoons ground cloves**

½ **nutmeg, grated**

6 **lb. joint of beef: topside, round, or brisket, boned and rolled**

½ **cup sea salt**

lamb with quince and cinnamon

This is based on an autumnal recipe from Corfu. The cut of lamb should be slightly fatty, to contrast with the sharp acidity of the fruit.

Cook the onions in the oil until they start to color. Add the pieces of lamb and brown all over. Then add just enough hot water to come level with the meat, adding cinnamon, salt, and pepper. Bring to a boil, cover, and simmer gently for 1 hour. Then add the sliced quinces and the sugar; cover again and cook for another 30 minutes, or until both lamb and quinces are tender. This is good served with a grain dish, such as rice or couscous, rather than with potatoes.

Serves 4

8 oz. onions, sliced
2 tablespoons olive oil
2 lb. middle end of neck of lamb, cut into pieces
1 teaspoon ground cinnamon
1 lb. quinces, peeled, cored, and thickly sliced
1 teaspoon sugar
salt and black pepper

Moroccan lamb tagine

1 Toss the lamb in seasoned flour and brown in the olive oil, stirring often. Using a slotted spoon, transfer the lamb to a plate. Put the sliced vegetables into the same pan and cook them gently for 4–5 minutes, stirring often, until they are lightly colored. Add the ginger toward the end of the time. Return the lamb to the pan.
2 Warm the saffron in a large metal spoon, moving it around over a gentle heat for about 30 seconds; then pound it in a mortar. Heat the stock and add 2 tablespoons to the saffron; leave to infuse for a few minutes while you add the rest of the stock to the lamb, adding salt and black pepper to taste. Then add the saffron infusion to the lamb, cover the pan and simmer for 1 hour. Finally, add the chopped apricots — they do not need soaking — and cook for another 15 minutes. Adjust the seasoning, adding lemon juice to taste, and serve with a grain dish — couscous or basmati rice, or a wild rice mixture — and a green salad.

Serves 4

1½ lb. boneless lamb (½ a boned leg or shoulder), cubed
seasoned flour
3 tablespoons olive oil
2 onions, sliced
2 green peppers, deseeded and cut in strips
1 head fennel, sliced
1 teaspoon ground ginger
½ teaspoon saffron threads
2½ cups chicken or veal stock
¾ cup dried apricots, chopped
1–2 tablespoons lemon juice
sea salt and black pepper

lamb couscous

This is not nearly as much trouble to make as it looks and is truly a wonderful dish.

1 Mix the ground coriander, cumin, harissa or chili powder, sea salt, and black pepper into the tomato purée, then rub the resulting paste all over the pieces of lamb. Leave for 1–2 hours.

2 Next prepare the couscous; put it in a bowl and pour 2½ cups cold water over it. Leave for 10 minutes, then stir with a wooden spoon, breaking up any lumps, and sprinkle the 2 teaspoons olive oil over it. Pour the couscous into the top part of a *couscousier*; if you don't have one, line a colander or large strainer with cheesecloth and pour the couscous into it.

3 In the bottom of the *couscousier* or in a large pan that will hold the strainer nicely, heat the 4 tablespoons olive oil and brown the pieces of lamb slowly, allowing about 10 minutes. Then add enough hot water to cover the lamb, and bring to a boil. Keep boiling steadily for 30 minutes, then add the onions, leeks, carrots, and turnips, adding more boiling water to come level with the vegetables. Add salt and pepper to taste. Now place the couscous over the lamb and cover with a lid. Bring back to a boil and cook steadily for another 30 minutes, then add the zucchinis. Add the tomatoes and the peas 15 minutes later, and cook for a final 15 minutes. By now the lamb should have been cooking for 1½ hours and the couscous for 1 hour; both should be ready at the same time.

4 Shortly before serving, toast the saffron threads by holding them in a large metal spoon over a gentle heat, shaking them slightly, for about 30 seconds. Then pound them in a mortar. To serve, pour the couscous onto a large platter, breaking up any lumps that have formed. Lift the vegetables out of the sauce with a slotted spoon and lay them on the bed of couscous. Scatter the garbanzos over them, and the torn cilantro leaves, if using. Lay the pieces of lamb on a separate dish. Add 2 tablespoons of the lamb sauce to the saffron in the mortar. Pound a few times, just enough to mix, then pour back into the sauce. Serve the sauce separately, with a small dish of Hot Sauce I or II also on the table.

Serves 4 to 6

---

1 teaspoon ground coriander
½ tablespoon ground cumin
½ teaspoon Harissa (see page 59) or
  chili powder
2 tablespoons tomato purée
3 lb. middle end of neck of lamb,
  unboned and cut in large pieces
4 tablespoons olive oil
4 oz. pickling onions, peeled
6 oz. thin leeks, cut in chunks
6 oz. small carrots, cut in 4 lengthwise
6 oz. small turnips, cut in 4
8 oz. small zucchinis, cut in
  thick chunks
6 oz. tomatoes, skinned and cut in 4
4 oz. peas, shelled
sea salt and black pepper

Couscous:
2⅔ cups couscous
2 teaspoons olive oil

To garnish:
½ teaspoon saffron threads
⅓ cup canned garbanzos, heated
2 tablespoons cilantro leaves, torn
  in pieces (optional)
Hot Sauce I or II (see page 185)

lambs' tongues
with mustard sauce

1 Wash the tongues well under cold running water and then scrub them with a stiff brush. Put them in a pan and add the sliced onion, leek, carrot, and celery, together with the bay leaf and seasonings. Pour on enough cold chicken stock to just cover them, and bring slowly to a boil. Simmer, covered, for 1½ hours, until they are tender when pierced with a skewer. Drain the vegetables in a colander, reserving the stock.

2 As soon as they are cool enough to handle, skin the tongues, using a small, sharp knife; keep them warm while you make the mustard sauce, using the stock the tongues have cooked in and omitting the dill weed. Serve the tongues on a platter with a little of the mustard sauce spooned over them, sprinkled with chopped parsley. Serve the rest of the sauce separately, and accompany the tongues with boiled new potatoes and a green vegetable.

Serves 4

8 lambs' tongues
I onion, thickly sliced
I leek, thickly sliced
I carrot, thickly sliced
I celery stalk, thickly sliced
I bay leaf
2 teaspoons sea salt
10 black peppercorns
3¾–4⅜ cups chicken stock
Hot Mustard Sauce (see page 188),
  omitting the dill weed
2 tablespoons chopped parsley, to
  garnish

boiled bacon
with juniper berry sauce

3½ lb. unsmoked back bacon, in 1
  piece
1 onion, halved
3 cloves
1 carrot, halved
1 celery stalk, halved
2 bay leaves
10 black peppercorns
1¼ cups strong dry cider

Sauce:
1¼ cups bacon stock
2 tablespoons butter
1 shallot, chopped
10 juniper berries, roughly crushed in
  a mortar
1½ tablespoons all-purpose flour
¼ cup light cream
black pepper

1 Unsmoked bacon should not need soaking prior to cooking. (If you are using smoked bacon, soak it in cold water overnight in order to reduce the salt content.) Put the bacon in a casserole and cover generously with cold water. Bring slowly to a boil, removing any scum as it rises to the surface. When the water is clear, add the onion halves stuck with the cloves, the halved carrot, celery, bay leaves, and peppercorns; salt will not be needed. Pour on the cider and bring back to a boil, then simmer gently for 1½ hours, or 30 minutes per 1 lb. When the time is up, remove the bacon; cover with foil and a cloth to keep warm.

2 Strain the stock and measure 1¼ cups for the sauce. Melt the butter, add the chopped shallot and juniper berries, and cook gently for 3 minutes. Then add the flour and cook for 1 minute more. Pour on the heated bacon stock, bring to a boil and simmer for 3 minutes. Then add the cream and adjust the seasoning. Pour into a sauceboat to serve, with the bacon cut in fairly thick slices. Accompany with a purée of potatoes and some simply boiled vegetables, such as carrots or cabbage.

Note: A large piece of ham may be used instead of the bacon. Simply adjust the cooking time accordingly, and ask advice from the supplier about whether or not to soak the ham prior to cooking.

Serves 6

spiced meatballs

These highly spiced meatballs are best made on a small scale, for serving with drinks or as part of a mixed hors-d'oeuvre. If making on a larger scale, reduce the spices by a third. Buy your lamb freshly ground by the butcher, or buy a lean cut and chop it at home in a food processor.

½ oz. dry white bread, crust
  removed, torn in pieces
3 tablespoons milk
1½ cups ground lamb
2 teaspoons sea salt
1½ tablespoons olive oil
1 red onion, finely chopped
1 garlic clove, chopped
2 teaspoons ground allspice
1 teaspoon cinnamon
black pepper

For frying:
2 tablespoons butter
1½ tablespoons sunflower oil

1 Soak the bread in the milk for 5 minutes, squeeze dry. Mix it into the lamb with the salt. In a pan, heat the oil and cook the onion for 5 minutes, then add the garlic and spices. Cook for another 3–4 minutes, stirring, remove from the heat and stir the onion, garlic, and spices into the lamb, mixing well with a spoon, then with the hands. Fry a small ball in a clean pan to gauge the seasoning. Form the mixture into balls weighing about ½ oz. each.

2 Fry over a high heat for 4–5 minutes in a mixture of butter and oil, and serve soon after making. Serve hot, or warm with drinks, or as a first course, accompanied by hard-boiled eggs, asparagus, and Cold Mustard Sauce (see page 188).

Makes about 24 small meatballs; serves 4 to 6 in either of the ways suggested above.

spareribs in barbecue sauce

Be sure to get spareribs in racks for broiling.

1 Start 1 day in advance. To make the sauce, soak the chopped chilies for 10 minutes in 4 tablespoons boiling water, then drain, reserving the water, and chop them again. Put them in a small mill with half their soaking water and grind to a paste. Mix this with the tomato purée and vinegar. Cook the chopped onion slowly in the oil, allowing 5–10 minutes for it to start to change color. Then stir in the chili mixture, adding 1 cup heated stock, the honey, mustard, garlic, bay leaf, spices, and seasonings. Simmer for 15 minutes, covered, stirring from time to time. Add more stock if the sauce becomes too thick. Leave to cool overnight.

2 Next day spread about half the sauce over the racks of ribs, reserving the rest for later. Leave them to marinate for 3–4 hours. Shortly before serving, line the broiler pan with foil and heat the broiler to its hottest. Lay the racks of ribs on the foil and broil them for 15 minutes on each side, turning them around and basting with the sauce occasionally. Divide them into single ribs to serve, piled on a flat dish. Pour any remaining sauce into a food processor, adding enough of the remaining stock to thin it, and process until blended. Reheat and serve in a sauceboat, with the ribs.

Serves 6 as a first course, or 4 as a light main dish; no vegetables are required.

3 lb. pork spareribs, in racks

Barbecue sauce:
2 dried chilies, deseeded and roughly chopped
3 tablespoons tomato purée
4 tablespoons white wine vinegar
1 onion, chopped
3 tablespoons light olive oil
about 1¼ cups chicken stock, heated
2 teaspoons clear honey
2 teaspoons Dijon mustard
1 large garlic clove, crushed
1 small bay leaf, crumbled
½ teaspoon ground coriander
½ teaspoon ground cumin
sea salt and black pepper

spicy pork sausages

A useful gadget like a small pump can be bought for filling sausage skins, and some food mixers have their own attachment for this purpose. Failing these, you can fill the skins by hand or ask a friendly butcher to do it for you. The skins, or casings, are made from the small intestines of the pig or sheep, and some butchers will let you have them.

1 Separate the fat from the belly of pork and cut it in small cubes by hand. Cut the rest in small chunks and put it in the food processor with the lean pork. (Alternatively, they can be put through a grinder.) Do not process for too long, for the texture should be fairly coarse, not reduced to a purée. Transfer the ground meat to a large bowl.

2 Soak the bread in the milk for 5 minutes, then squeeze dry and add to the ground pork with the cubed pork fat, garlic, and chilies. Crush the juniper berries with the black and green peppercorns, and stir into the mixture with the sea salt. Fry a small ball of meat in a frying pan to gauge the seasonings; add more salt or pepper as required. Then fill your casings. The sausages may be broiled, fried, or baked in a preheated oven, 350°F, for 30–35 minutes, and served with Hot Mustard Sauce (see page 188).

Makes about 1½ lb.

I lb. belly of pork

8 oz. lean pork, from the leg, cut in small chunks

I½ cups soft white breadcrumbs

4 tablespoons milk

2 garlic cloves, finely chopped

2 red chilies, deseeded and finely chopped

10 juniper berries

6 black peppercorns

10 green peppercorns

2 teaspoons sea salt

sausage skins or casings

broiled pork steaks
with caraway seeds

Some butchers and supermarkets sell pork steaks, cut about ½ inch thick, like a thin pork chop without the bone.

4 pork steaks

Marinade:
3 tablespoons light soy sauce
3 tablespoons *sake* or dry vermouth
**1½ tablespoons finely chopped
  shallots**
**1 tablespoon caraway seeds or
  sesame seeds**
black pepper

1 Lay the pork steaks in a shallow dish. Mix together the soy sauce and *sake* or dry vermouth, adding the chopped shallots. Spoon over the pork steaks, adding some freshly ground black pepper. Leave to marinate for 1–2 hours, turning over once or twice.

2 Heat the broiler, lay the pork steaks on the rack and scatter half the caraway or sesame seeds over them. Broil at a fairly low heat for about 5 minutes, then turn them over and baste with the soy sauce and *sake* or dry vermouth marinade. Scatter the remaining seeds over the second side and broil for another 4–5 minutes. Serve the pork steaks immediately, for broiled food soon becomes dry.

Serves 4 with a purée of potatoes and a green salad.

vegetables

To add zest to vegetables, serve them with mustard seed butter. To make the butter, toast 1 tablespoon black mustard seeds in a dry skillet for 2–3 minutes, then put in a food processor with $7/8$ cup sweet butter, $1/2$ teaspoon sea salt, a few turns of the black-pepper mill and $1/2$ tablespoon lemon juice. Process until blended, then chill for 1 hour to firm. Form into roll and wrap in foil, chill again or freeze. To serve, cut in thick slices and lay over boiled vegetables or broiled beef steaks.

eggplant & cumin purée

1 Broil the eggplants for about 25 minutes, turning at regular intervals, until they are soft when pierced with a skewer. Then remove from the heat and leave to cool. Toast the cumin seeds in a dry skillet over low heat for 1–2 minutes, then grind in a small mill or pound in a mortar.

2 When the eggplants are cool enough to handle, cut them in half lengthwise and scoop out the flesh. Squeeze it to release the moisture, then chop it roughly by hand and mash it with a fork, adding the cumin. (Do not use a food processor, as the purée should not be too smooth.) Mix the oil and lemon juice, and stir into the eggplant, mashing until blended, then add the crushed garlic, sea salt, and black pepper. Stir in the yogurt and adjust the seasoning, adding more lemon juice, salt, and pepper as required. Sprinkle with chopped parsley and serve as a first course with lightly toasted pita bread.

Makes just over 1 lb.; serves 4.

2 lb. eggplants
½ tablespoon cumin seeds
2 tablespoons olive oil
4 tablespoons lemon juice
1 large garlic clove, crushed
⅝ cup yogurt
sea salt and black pepper
1 tablespoon finely chopped flat-leaf
   parsley, to garnish

braised celeriac with cumin & coriander

1 Heat the oil in a large deep pan. Cut the celeriac quarters in thin slices. Do not do this in advance or they will discolor, spoiling the look of the dish. Turn them in the hot oil for 6 minutes, adding the cumin and coriander toward the end. Then add the heated stock, salt, and pepper, and bring to a boil. Cover the pan and cook gently for 45 minutes, or 15 minutes in a pressure cooker. When the time is up, drain the celeriac and keep it warm while you boil the sauce to reduce slightly. Then pour the sauce over the celeriac in its dish, and sprinkle with chopped cilantro, chervil, or parsley.

2 If making as part of a cold Braised Pheasant with Lemon Grass (see page 131), omit the spices and the herb.

Serves 4 to 6

2 tablespoons sunflower oil
1 celeriac, peeled and cut in 4
1 teaspoon ground cumin
1 teaspoon ground coriander
1¼ cups chicken stock,
   heated
sea salt and black pepper
1½ tablespoons chopped fresh
   cilantro leaves, chervil or flat-leaf
   parsley, to garnish

saffron vegetable stew

4 small carrots, cut in ½ inch chunks

4 tablespoons olive oil

3 small leeks, cut in ½ inch slices

1 head fennel, halved and thinly
sliced

3 zucchinis, cut in ½ inch slices

2 bunches large scallions, trimmed

2 tomatoes, skinned and cut in
quarters

¼ teaspoon saffron threads

1¼ cups chicken or vegetable stock,
heated

salt and black pepper

1 Drop the carrots into lightly salted boiling water and cook for 3 minutes, then drain. Heat the oil in a heavy pan and drop in the sliced leeks, parboiled carrots, and sliced fennel. Cook gently for 4 minutes, then add the sliced zucchinis and cook for another 4 minutes. Now add the whole scallions and quartered tomatoes, and cook for another 2–3 minutes.

2 Steep the saffron in 3 tablespoons of the hot stock for 5 minutes, then add to the pan with the rest of the stock, salt, and black pepper. Bring to a boil, cover the pan and simmer gently for 30 minutes. Serve hot, with couscous that has been steamed over chicken or vegetable stock, or with basmati rice.

Serves 4, or 6 with other dishes.

carrots and zucchinis
with sesame

Sesame-flavored dishes like this one go well with roasted and broiled poultry, and other vegetables. I like to eat this dish with brown rice and a dash of light soy sauce.

Heat the oil in a wok-shaped pan and throw in the carrots. Toss for 3 minutes, then add the zucchinis and continue to toss for another 3 minutes, adding sea salt and black pepper. Finally, add a dash of sesame oil — not too much, as it is very strong — and stir in the lightly toasted sesame seeds.

Serves 4

Variation: Instead of slicing the vegetables, use a swivel-blade vegetable peeler to cut them downward in long, thin slivers. Use 4 oz. each of carrots and zucchinis and 2 tablespoons oil. Cook the carrots for 4 minutes, the zucchinis for 2 minutes.

Serves 2 to 3

2½ tablespoons sunflower oil

8 oz. carrots, cut in thin diagonal slices

2 large zucchinis, cut in thin diagonal slices

a few shakes sesame oil

1½ tablespoons sesame seeds, lightly toasted

sea salt and black pepper

buttered leeks
with sweet corn

This goes well with simple dishes such as broiled lamb cutlets, broiled steaks, roasted or broiled chicken, brown rice, and other vegetable dishes.

Cook the leeks gently in the butter and oil for 10 minutes, adding the chopped chili(es) after a moment or two. Meanwhile, cut the kernels off the corn cobs with a sharp knife, then scrape the juices from the cobs into a saucer with the back of the knife. Add the kernels and juices to the leeks with the chopped tomatoes and continue to cook for 5 minutes, adding sea salt and black pepper. When the time is up, test the vegetables to make sure they are tender, taste for seasoning, then stir in the chopped cilantro, if using, and serve.

Serves 4

3 leeks, cut in half and sliced

¼ cup butter

1 tablespoon sunflower oil

1–2 red chilies, deseeded and finely chopped

2 ears corn

3 tomatoes, skinned and coarsely chopped

3 tablespoons chopped cilantro leaves (optional)

sea salt and black pepper

corn fritters with salsa fresca

1 Cut the kernels off the corn with a sharp knife, then scrape the juices into a bowl with the back of the knife. Weigh the kernels; you should have about 8 oz. Add them to the juices in the bowl, with the cream, flour, baking powder, sugar, salt, and pepper. Mix well.

2 Heat a flat skillet or griddle until very hot. Rub all over with a buttered piece of paper, then drop the corn mixture on, using a large spoon. Flatten the mounds of corn slightly, keeping them in a fairly even, round shape and allowing little holes to develop here and there. Lower the heat and cook for 3–4 minutes on each side, until nicely browned. Slide on to paper towels, then transfer to a heated dish and keep warm while you cook the rest. Serve as soon as possible, with the salsa.

Serves 4 as a first course.

3–4 ears corn, depending on size
4 tablespoons heavy cream
2 tablespoons sifted cake flour
½ teaspoon baking powder
½ teaspoon sugar
sea salt and black pepper
Salsa Fresca (see page 191), made in advance, to serve

spinach purée with mace

This pretty green purée is excellent served with poached or fried fish, fish cakes, chicken, lamb cutlets, or hard-boiled eggs.

1 Cook the spinach in lightly salted boiling water for 4–5 minutes, depending on whether it is young and tender or older and coarser. (Tender summer spinach will need only 4 minutes.) Drain it well, squeezing out most of the water with the back of a wooden spoon. It does not need to be completely dry, as the sauce will absorb a little extra liquid. Put the spinach in a food processor while you make the sauce.

2 Melt the butter, add the flour, and cook gently for 1 minute, stirring. Add the mace and continue to cook for 1 minute longer. Then pour on the cream, stirring, and bring back to a boil. Simmer very gently for 3 minutes, then pour onto the spinach in the processor, adding lots of sea salt and black pepper. Process to a smooth purée, then pour into a pan and reheat gently, tasting for seasoning.

Note: Nutmeg may be used instead of mace, if preferred.

Serves 4 to 6

2 lb. spinach
2 tablespoons butter
2 teaspoons all-purpose flour
1½ tablespoons ground mace
1¾ cups light cream
sea salt and black pepper

zucchini fritters
with Romesco sauce

Smoky Salsa (see page 187) or Salsa Fresca (see page 191) may be substituted for the Romesco Sauce if preferred.

Romesco Sauce (see page 189)
10 oz. zucchinis, unpeeled
oil, for frying
2 lemons, cut in quarters, to garnish

Batter:
1 cup cake flour, sifted
a pinch of salt
2 tablespoons sunflower oil
⅝ cup soda water or sparkling
  mineral water
1 egg white, stiffly beaten

1 First make the romesco sauce, then make the batter. Sift the flour into a food processor with the salt. Process, adding the oil through the lid, then the soda water or sparkling mineral water. When the batter is smooth, pour it into a large bowl and fold in the stiffly beaten egg white.

2 Half fill a wok or wide pan with frying oil and heat to 360°F or until a cube of bread browns in 30 seconds. While the oil is heating, cut the unpeeled zucchinis in slices about ⅛ inch thick. When the oil has reached the correct temperature, dip each zucchini slice in the batter, scraping off any excess on the side of the bowl, and drop into the wok or pan. Fry just a few at a time; don't crowd them. They will take only about 2 minutes on each side to become light golden brown and crisp. Then lift them out and drain on paper towels while you cook the next batch. Transfer each batch to a heated dish and keep warm until all are done. Serve as soon as they are ready, with romesco sauce and quartered lemons.

Serves 4 as a first course.

broiled
tomatoes
with polenta

1 teaspoon salt

1 cup instant polenta

8 tomatoes

2 bunches scallions, coarsely chopped

2 garlic cloves, finely chopped

1 inch square fresh root
  ginger, peeled and finely chopped

2 small red chilies, deseeded and
  finely chopped

2 tablespoons chopped basil

1 cup orange juice

1 cup olive oil

sea salt and black pepper

To garnish:

3–4 oz. arugula or watercress

2 tablespoons extra virgin olive oil

To make this successfully, you need a small loaf pan or a rectangular dish or mold.

1 Put $3\frac{1}{8}$ cups water in a pan, add the salt and bring to a boil. Shake in the polenta gradually, then stir constantly while it comes back to a boil. Continue to boil steadily for 5 minutes, stirring all the time, then remove from the heat and pour into a loaf pan, measuring about 6 x $3\frac{1}{2}$ x $2\frac{1}{2}$ inches deep. Leave to cool and set for a few hours or overnight.

2 Later, turn the polenta out of the pan and cut in slices $\frac{1}{2}$ inch thick. Cut off the tops of the tomatoes and hollow out most of the seeds and juice. Turn the tomatoes upside down to drain for a bit, then wipe them dry with paper towels and sprinkle the insides with sea salt and black pepper. Mix the chopped scallions, garlic, ginger, chilies, and basil, then use the mixture to fill the tomatoes. Pour 1 tablespoon orange juice and 1 tablespoon olive oil over each.

3 Shortly before serving, broil the tomatoes for about 8 minutes, until soft. Heat a ridged cast-iron broiler pan on top of the range until it is very hot, then brush it lightly with oil and cook the polenta slices until they have developed brownish-black stripes. Lay the arugula or watercress around a flat dish and drizzle the virgin olive oil over it. Lay the broiled tomatoes on the green leaves with the broiled polenta slices all around.

Serves 4 as a light main dish, needing no other accompaniment.

grated zucchinis
and kohlrabi

When kohlrabi is not obtainable, use turnips or celeriac. When none of these are in season, simply double the amount of zucchinis.

Process the tomatoes briefly in a blender or food processor, then set aside. Heat the sunflower oil in a wok and cook the garlic, chili(es) and ginger for 2 minutes, tossing. Then add the grated kohlrabi and cook for another 2 minutes. Pour in the zucchinis and continue to cook for another 2–3 minutes, adding salt and pepper. Then stir in the puréed tomatoes and chopped basil. Serve immediately over brown basmati rice.

Serves 3 to 4 as a light main dish.

2 tomatoes, skinned, deseeded, and roughly chopped
3 tablespoons sunflower oil
2 tablespoons finely chopped garlic
1–2 red chilies, deseeded and finely chopped
2 tablespoons finely chopped fresh root ginger
8 oz. kohlrabi, coarsely grated
12 oz. zucchinis, coarsely grated
2 tablespoons basil, torn in pieces
sea salt and black pepper

spicy black beans

This is best served alone, as a dish in its own right, rather than as a vegetable accompaniment to meat or fish.

1 Cover the beans with plenty of fresh cold water. Bring slowly to a boil, then boil quite fast for 10 minutes. Lower the heat and simmer for about 1 hour or until the beans are soft but not broken, testing often after about 30 minutes.

2 Drain the beans, reserving the liquid. Heat the sunflower oil and fry the red onion for 4 minutes, then add the chopped garlic and the three spices. Cook for another 2 minutes, stirring, then pour on the heated stock and simmer gently for 10–15 minutes, half covered. Finally, stir in the cooked beans and reheat, stirring often and seasoning to taste with salt and black pepper. Just before serving, stir in the lime juice, if using. Turn into a serving dish and top with sour cream, sprinkled with chopped cilantro leaves; or serve the garnishes separately in bowls at the table.

Serves 4

1⅓ cups dried black (or red) kidney beans, soaked overnight
2 tablespoons sunflower oil
½ red onion, thinly sliced
2 garlic cloves, finely chopped
1 teaspoon ground coriander
1 teaspoon ground cumin
¼ teaspoon chili powder or cayenne
⅝ cup chicken or vegetable stock, heated
2 tablespoons lime juice (optional)
sea salt and black pepper

To garnish:
⅝ cup sour cream
1½ tablespoons chopped cilantro leaves

mushrooms with coriander

This dish can be made with different sorts of mixed mushrooms, or with a single variety. For reasons of cost, I tend to use two-thirds farmed chestnut or field mushrooms, and one-third more exotic ones, such as shiitake, morel or cep, to add interest.

1 Wipe the mushrooms with a damp cloth and cut the larger ones in halves or quarters. Heat the oil and fry the onion for 5 minutes, then add the garlic and cook for another 2 minutes. Crush the coriander seeds and peppercorns roughly in a mortar and add to the pan; cook gently for 2–3 minutes, then add the exotic mushrooms. (These usually take slightly longer to cook than the common ones.)
2 Cook gently for 2–3 minutes, stirring often, then add the other mushrooms. Stir for 3 minutes, or until the mushrooms start to wilt, then heat the stock and pour on. Bring to a boil and simmer for 4–6 minutes, or until the mushrooms are cooked, adding plenty of sea salt. Boil for a moment or two to reduce the liquid slightly, then add the soy sauce and about two-thirds of the fresh cilantro. Turn into a serving dish, scatter the rest of the fresh cilantro over the top and serve with brown rice, buckwheat, or other grain or vegetable dishes.

Serves 4

- 8 oz. chestnut or field mushrooms, stems trimmed
- 4 oz. shiitake, ceps (porcini) or morels, stems trimmed
- 3 tablespoons olive oil
- ½ red onion, finely chopped
- 2 garlic cloves, finely chopped
- 1 teaspoon whole coriander seeds
- 1 teaspoon whole Jamaica peppercorns or mixed red and green, or black and white, peppercorns
- ⅝ cup game, chicken, or vegetable stock
- ½ teaspoon sea salt
- ½ teaspoon light soy sauce
- 3 tablespoons very roughly chopped cilantro leaves

zucchinis with coriander

This fresh-tasting and delicious dish is simple and quick to make.

Heat the butter and oil in a wok or similar-shaped pan. Throw in the coarsely grated zucchinis, add the coriander, and toss briskly while they cook. They will take only about 2–3 minutes. Then add salt and black pepper to taste, and serve.

Serves 4

- 2 tablespoons butter
- 2 tablespoons sunflower oil
- 4 zucchinis, unpeeled and coarsely grated
- 1 teaspoon ground coriander
- sea salt and black pepper

spicy salad

In Egypt, a spicy mixed salad is made by adding shatah, a pounded chili pepper, to the salad dressing. The same effect can be achieved by using chili powder, cayenne, or Tabasco sauce.

Mix the chopped tomatoes, cucumber, and onion with the sprigs of watercress. Mix the oil and lemon juice, adding the chili powder, cayenne, or Tabasco sauce to taste. Pour over the salad and mix thoroughly.

Note: This salad is best served alone or as a part of a mixed hors-d'oeuvre, rather than as an accompaniment to a main dish.

Serves 4

12 oz. tomatoes, skinned and
 chopped
½ cucumber, unpeeled and chopped
½ large mild onion, chopped
1 bunch watercress, cut into small
 sprigs

Dressing:
5 tablespoons olive oil
2 tablespoons lemon juice
⅛ teaspoon chili powder or cayenne,
 or a dash of Tabasco sauce

pasta, potatoes, rice, pastry, and grains

Pasta tossed with garlic, olive oil, and hot red pepper flakes makes a delightful dish for an informal supper. Hot red pepper flakes can be fierce, so add them gradually, to taste.

Yemeni spiced rice

During a recent trip to Yemen, I ate this excellent dish every day for 2½ weeks, accompanied by wonderful flat bread and vegetables stewed in oil. The simpler the restaurant, the better it was.

1 Cook the chopped onion slowly in the oil for 4 minutes, then add the cardamom seeds and currants and cook for another 4 minutes, stirring often. Then stir in the freshly cooked rice and continue stirring until coated with oil.

2 Add the sea salt and black pepper, and continue to stir until well heated. Serve as it is, or with a garnish of bay leaf and cinnamon stick, crushed in a mortar, with extra cardomom seeds scattered over it if you wish.

Serves 4, with oily dishes of lamb, chicken, or vegetables.

½ cup chopped onion
2 tablespoons sunflower oil
10 cardamom pods, shelled (about
  ½ teaspoon seeds)
1 tablespoon currants
2¼ cups freshly cooked basmati rice
sea salt and pepper

Garnish (optional):
1 bay leaf, crumbled
1 stick cinnamon, broken and
  crushed
¼ teaspoon cardamom seeds

couscous croquettes

1 Put the couscous in a bowl and pour 1 cup cold water over it. Leave for 10 minutes, then tip into the top part of a *couscousier* or a strainer lined with cheesecloth. Set the strainer over a saucepan of simmering vegetable stock and cook gently, covered, for 30 minutes, taking care that the strainer does not touch the stock, for the couscous must cook in the steam, not in the liquid. Transfer the steamed couscous to a bowl.

2 Heat half the oil in a skillet and cook the sliced scallions in it for 2–3 minutes, then add the ginger and the chili and cook for another 1–2 minutes. Then stir the onion mixture into the steamed couscous and mix well.

3 Add the *fromage frais* to the beaten egg and beat again, then stir into the couscous, adding the chopped cilantro leaves and plenty of sea salt and black pepper. Form the mixture into 8 round patties and chill for several hours or overnight to firm.

4 Shortly before serving, heat the remaining oil in a wide non-stick skillet and fry the croquettes until they are nicely colored all over. Drain on paper towels and serve with a bowl of yogurt, and a tomato-and-cucumber salad.

Serves 4

1 cup couscous
1⅞ cups vegetable stock, heated
3 tablespoons sunflower oil
½ bunch scallions, sliced
1 inch square fresh root ginger,
  peeled and finely chopped
1 small red chili, deseeded and finely
  chopped
4 tablespoons *fromage frais* (or substitute neufchâtel cheese
1 egg, beaten
2 tablespoons chopped
  cilantro leaves
sea salt and black pepper

dhal

Dhal is the everyday food of much of India, the equivalent of bread, pasta, and potatoes in the West. Shops selling the various dhals and spices such as asafoetida are few and far between outside India, but this recipe works well using Western equivalents. Asafoetida should be included whenever possible, as it makes foods that are high in vegetable protein, such as lentil or bean porridges, much easier to digest.

1⅓ cups *masoor dhal* (split red lentils) or *channa dal* (yellow split peas)

½ teaspoon ground turmeric

½ teaspoon chili powder

I teaspoon salt

I teaspoon vegetable oil

To garnish:

3 tablespoons sunflower oil

⅛ teaspoon asafoetida (optional)

½ teaspoon cumin seeds (preferably black cumin)

½ teaspoon hot red pepper flakes

2 tablespoons roughly chopped cilantro leaves

1 Pick over the dried lentils or peas carefully, discarding all foreign bodies, such as bits of stone. Wash the lentils or peas well under cold running water, then put in a saucepan with the turmeric, chili powder, and salt. Add 2½ cups cold water and 1 teaspoon oil, which will stop the water from frothing up and forming a thick scum. Bring to a boil, half cover the pan, and simmer for 10–20 minutes, stirring often toward the end of the cooking to prevent the dhal from sticking. When the dhal is ready, cover the pan completely and remove from the heat.

2 Just before serving, make the garnish. (This is called a *tarka* or *bageer* in India.) Heat the oil in a small skillet. When it is very hot, put in the asafoetida, if using, and fry for a few seconds, just until it changes color. Then add the cumin seeds and hot red pepper flakes and cook for a few seconds longer, then throw in the chopped cilantro leaves and remove from the heat. Pour the garnish over the hot dhal and stir until blended. Serve immediately.

Note: This dish can also be made with green split peas, whole green lentils, or whole mung beans. If using whole lentils or mung beans, use an extra 1¼ cups water and let boil for 35–40 minutes.

Serves 3 to 4 as a simple meal with basmati rice, yogurt, and a fruit chutney; serves 4 to 6 as an accompaniment to a meat or vegetable curry.

potatoes with black beans

This is based on an Indian filling for samosas that I prefer to use as a dish in its own right. It can also be used as a filling for Spring Rolls (see page 176).

1 Cover the beans with plenty of fresh water and bring to a boil. Cook hard for 10 minutes, then lower the heat and simmer for about 1 hour, or 20 minutes in a pressure cooker, until the beans are soft without being mushy. Add the vegetable stock powder, if using, toward the end of the cooking. Drain well.

2 Boil the unskinned potatoes in lightly salted water. Remove from the heat as soon as they are cooked; don't overcook them whatever you do. Drain, peel, and dice them in ¼ inch pieces. Heat the oils in a skillet and cook the chopped onion for 5 minutes. Add the fenugreek and mustard seeds and continue to cook over low heat until the onion starts to brown. Then add the drained beans, ground cumin, sea salt, lemon juice, and ¼ cup water. Cook for 3–4 minutes, stirring constantly. Then stir in the chopped cilantro leaves. Serve hot or warm as part of a spread of vegetable dishes.

Serves 4 to 6 with other dishes.

½ **cup dried black (or red) kidney beans, soaked overnight**
½ **teaspoon vegetable stock powder (optional)**
1½ **lb. potatoes**
2 tablespoons olive oil
2 tablespoons sunflower oil
1 onion, finely chopped
1 teaspoon fenugreek seeds
1 teaspoon white mustard seeds
1 teaspoon cumin seeds, roasted and ground
2 teaspoons sea salt
2 tablespoons lemon juice
3–4 tablespoons chopped fresh cilantro leaves

cold spiced noodles

1 Heat the oil in the pan, add the sliced scallions, and cook for 3 minutes; then add the crushed lemon grass and chopped chili. Stir over low heat for another 2–3 minutes, then set aside. Cook the noodles in lightly salted boiling water for 2–3 minutes, then drain well. Put them back in the pan and reheat, adding the scallion and chili mixture, the *passato*, and sea salt and black pepper to taste. Cook very gently for 3–4 minutes, stirring often, then set aside. Remove the lemon grass before serving.

2 Serve at room temperature; if making in advance and storing in the refrigerator, be sure to take out 1 hour before serving.

Serves 4, or 6 with other dishes.

3 tablespoons sunflower oil
6 large scallions, thinly sliced
1 stalk lemon grass, crushed
1 red chili, deseeded and finely chopped
8 oz. very thin noodles (tagliolini)
½ **cup *Passato di Pomodoro* (see page 190), made in advance**
sea salt and black pepper

hot potato pastries

1 Put the oil in a pan with the red pepper flakes; warm for 3 minutes, set aside.

2 Boil the potatoes. Drain and skin them. Push through a medium food mill into a clean pan. Warm the milk and half the butter. Reheat the potatoes gently, adding the milk and butter and chili oil. Beat well, adding salt and pepper; set aside.

3 Melt the remaining butter. Take 1 sheet of pastry. Cover the rest of the pastry with a damp cloth. Lay the sheet out flat. Cut in rectangles measuring 2 x 10 inches. Brush with the melted butter and lay 1 heaped teaspoon of mashed potato on a narrow end of each one. Fold up the pastry in a triangular shape (see diagram), enclosing the potato filling. Brush the finished triangle all over with melted butter to seal. Repeat the process until all the filling has been used.

4 Lay the pastries on a lightly oiled cookie sheet and bake in a preheated oven, 350°F, for 15–18 minutes. Serve soon after baking.

Makes about 14; serves 4.

3 tablespoons virgin olive oil
½ teaspoon hot red pepper flakes
I lb. waxy potatoes
¼ cup milk
½ cup butter
about 5 sheets filo pastry
sea salt and black pepper

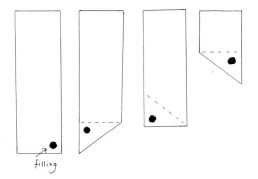

filling

saffron risotto

1 Toast the saffron threads in a dry skillet over very gentle heat for 10–15 seconds, then pound them in a mortar. Add 4 tablespoons of the heated stock and leave to infuse while you cook the risotto.

2 Fry the chopped shallot in the butter and oil for about 3 minutes, then add the rice and stir for another 2–3 minutes. Then pour on half the heated stock and allow to cook slowly, stirring often, until it has been absorbed. Have the rest of the stock already very hot, beside the heat. Now pour on half of it, adding the saffron-flavored stock and sea salt and black pepper. Continue to cook slowly, stirring frequently, until this stock is absorbed. Test the rice to see if it is tender; if not, add the remaining stock and continue cooking until all has been absorbed and the rice is tender. Serve immediately, with a bowl of grated Parmesan on the table.

Note: This dish takes about 25 minutes to cook from start to finish. It should be undertaken only when you are able to stay with it all the time.

Serves 4 as a first course.

½ teaspoon saffron threads
3⅛ cups chicken stock, heated
I shallot, finely chopped
2 tablespoons butter
I tablespoon olive oil
I cup arborio rice
sea salt and black pepper
freshly grated Parmesan cheese,
  to serve

This is a beautiful dish, with glowing, jewel-like colors.

1 Salt the eggplant slices on both sides and leave for 30 minutes. Then rinse off the salt, pat dry and brush with a little of the olive oil. Broil them, or cook on a ridged cast-iron broiler pan on top of the heat, until browned; then cut across in diagonal strips about 1 inch wide. Soak the chilies for 20 minutes in 4 tablespoons boiling water, then lift out the chilies and chop. Purée them with half their soaking water in a coffee mill or small blender. Cut the half onion in half again, then cut each piece across to make 4 chunky pieces. Divide the pieces into individual layers.

2 Heat 3 tablespoons olive oil in a heavy pan and add the onion pieces. Cook gently for 5 minutes, then add the whole garlic cloves and continue to cook gently for another 10 minutes, until the onion has softened without coloring.

3 Cut the skinned peppers across in broad diagonal strips, like the eggplants, and add to the onions with the chili purée. Add sea salt and black pepper, and cook for 5 minutes. Then add the strips of broiled eggplant and reheat gently together for 4–5 minutes. At the same time, cook the pasta in lightly salted boiling water for 4–5 minutes, or until tender, then drain. Add the chopped parsley to the vegetable mixture and serve over the pasta.

Serves 4

1 eggplant, cut in ½ inch thick slices
4–6 tablespoons olive oil
2 dried chilies, deseeded and stalks
   removed
½ large Spanish onion
6 large garlic cloves, peeled
1 red pepper, broiled, skinned,
   and deseeded
1 yellow pepper, broiled, skinned,
   and deseeded
13 oz. fettucine or other
   flat noodles
3 tablespoons flat-leaf parsley,
   chopped
sea salt and black pepper

pasta
with eggplant, peppers, and chilies

1 Make the pastry 1–2 hours in advance. Sift the flour and salt into a food processor or large bowl. Add the butter and process, or cut in, until the mixture resembles fine breadcrumbs. Now add the water gradually, continuing to process, or mix with the blade of a knife, until the dough starts to cling together. Turn onto a floured piece of plastic wrap, wrap and chill for 20 minutes.

2 Butter 6 tart pans measuring approximately 4 inches across and 1¾ inches deep. Divide the dough into 6 equal pieces and roll each one out to line a pan. Weigh down with foil and dried beans, and bake in a preheated oven, 375°F, for 5 minutes. Then remove the foil and beans. Make the glaze by beating the egg yolk with the milk, and brush this all over the pastry, and bake for another 6–8 minutes. Allow to cool.

3 Shortly before serving, make the filling. Add the mustard powder, cream, sea salt, and black pepper to the beaten eggs. Stir in about two-thirds of the grated Parmesan. Lay the halved tomatoes in the cases, cut sides up, and pour the egg mixture over them. Scatter the remaining grated cheese over the top and bake in a preheated oven, 350°F, for 15 minutes, until set and golden brown. These are best served immediately, but they are also good warm, or even cold.

Serves 6 as a first course.

Pastry:
2¼ cups cake flour
¼ teaspoon sea salt
½ cup butter, cut in small
   pieces
3–4 tablespoons iced water

Glaze:
1 egg yolk
1 tablespoon milk

Filling:
½ teaspoon mustard powder
⅝ cup heavy cream
2 eggs, beaten
¼ cup freshly grated
   Parmesan cheese
6 oz. cherry tomatoes, halved
sea salt and black pepper

tomato & mustard tarts

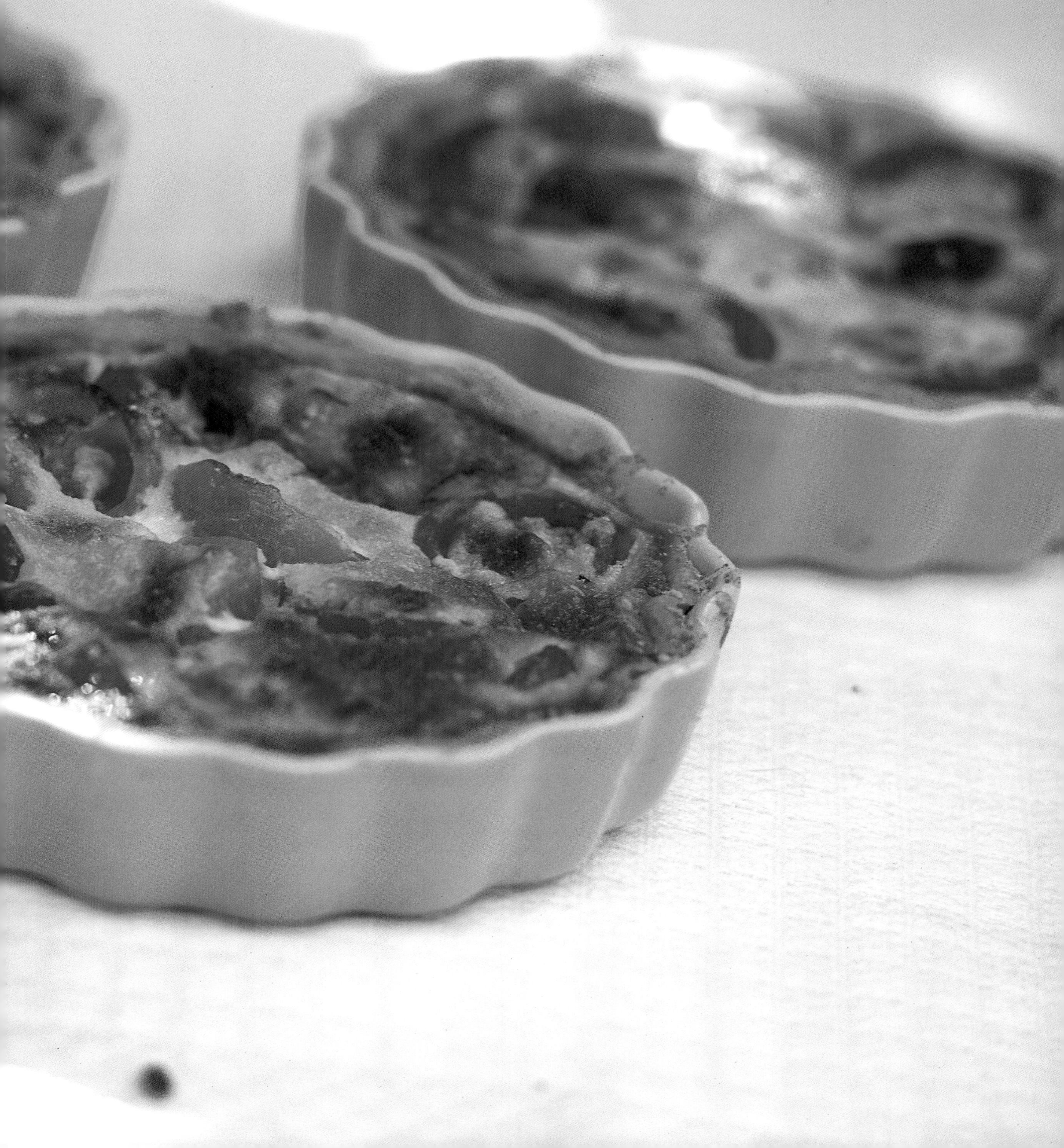

leek tart with mustard

1 Make the pastry 2–3 hours ahead. Sift the flour and salt in a food processor or bowl. Add the butter and process, or cut in, until the mixture resembles fine breadcrumbs. Add the water gradually, continuing to process or mix, until it starts to cling together. Turn onto floured plastic wrap, wrap and chill for 20 minutes.

2 Oil a 10 inch flan pan. Roll out the pastry to line it, weigh down with foil and dried or baking beans, and bake in a preheated oven, 400°F, for 8 minutes. Remove the foil and beans. Make the glaze by beating the egg yolk with the milk, and brush all over the pastry. Bake for 6 minutes more.

3 Cook the sliced leeks slowly in the butter until soft, some 10–12 minutes, then remove from the heat. Beat the eggs and egg yolk together, add the cream, mustard, and salt and pepper to taste. Stir in most of the cheese, reserving about 2 tablespoons.

4 About 45 minutes before serving, pour the filling into the pastry case, scatter the reserved cheese over the top, and bake in a preheated oven, 400°F, for 30 minutes, or until golden brown.

Serves 6 as a first course, or 4 as a main dish with a green salad.

Pastry:
3¼ cups cake flour
½ teaspoon salt
¾ cup butter, cut in small pieces
4–6 tablespoons iced water

Glaze:
I egg yolk
I tablespoon milk

Filling:
2 lb. leeks, trimmed and cut in half lengthwise and sliced
⅜ cup butter
2 eggs
I egg yolk
⅝ cup heavy cream
½ teaspoon mustard powder
2 oz. freshly grated Gruyère cheese
sea salt and black pepper

Viennese bread dumplings

1 Pour the milk over the pieces of bread roll. Leave for 10 minutes, then squeeze out and pull into smaller bits. Beat the melted butter into the egg, then stir in the soaked bread and parsley. Beat well. Add salt, pepper, and nutmeg; stir in the dry breadcrumbs. Continue to beat until well blended. Cover and leave for 15 minutes.

2 Make balls weighing about ½ oz. each out of the mixture; roll between the wet palms of your hands until smooth and well formed. Shortly before serving, drop them into a pan of lightly salted simmering water. Simmer for 5 minutes, then lift out with a slotted spoon and place 2–3 into each bowl of hot soup.

Note: I find the dumplings cling together much better when made 1 day in advance and left overnight in the refrigerator.

Makes about 18; serves 6.

¾–I cup milk
2 x I-day-old white bread rolls weighing about 2 oz. each, crust left on, torn into small pieces
3 tablespoons butter, just melted
I egg, beaten
2 tablespoons finely chopped parsley
freshly grated nutmeg
I cup soft white breadcrumbs
sea salt and black pepper

polenta cake
with tomato chili sauce

1 Heat 2½ cups of lightly salted water in a pan with a heavy base. As it approaches boiling point, start to shake in the polenta gradually, stirring all the time. When it starts to boil, lower the heat and simmer gently for 5 minutes, stirring often, until it becomes thick and smooth and comes away from the sides of the pan. Then pour it into a non-stick skillet to make a round cake about 1½ inches thick. Continue to cook gently for 10–15 minutes, until nicely browned underneath, while you make the sauce.

2 To serve, turn out the polenta cake onto a flat dish and cut in wedges, and put the tomato-chili sauce in a separate bowl.

Note: If you cannot get quick polenta, make as above allowing 40 minutes cooking.

Serves 4 as a light main dish with a green salad.

⅞ cup quick or instant polenta
salt
Tomato Chili Sauce (see page 184)

ginger dumplings

1 If using beef marrow, weigh it and make up to 3 tablespoons with butter, or use butter alone. Warm the fat(s) slightly, until just melted, in a bowl standing in a pan of hot water. Beat with a wooden spoon, then add the beaten egg gradually, beating all the time. Then add the salt and half the breadcrumbs, continuing to beat. Now add the ginger and cilantro or chervil. Finally, stir in the remaining breadcrumbs and beat until smooth. Cover the bowl with plastic wrap and let rest for 30 minutes.

2 Shortly before serving, form the dough into small balls not much bigger than your thumbnail, using a heaped teaspoon of the mixture at a time. When all are formed, drop them into a wide pan of lightly salted simmering water. Do not crowd them. Have the hot soup ready in bowls (see page 73), and put 2–3 dumplings into each bowl just before serving.

Makes about 18; serves 4 to 6.

3 tablespoons fat (beef marrow and/or butter), softened
1 egg, beaten
a pinch of salt
1 cup soft white breadcrumbs
1 teaspoon ground ginger, or peeled and grated fresh root ginger
2 tablespoons finely chopped fresh cilantro leaves or chervil

potatoes with
yogurt & cilantro

Try to include a black seed, whether onion, mustard, or poppy, as this adds immensely to the appearance of the dish.

1 Cook the potatoes in lightly salted boiling water until just tender, then drain. When they are cool enough to handle, skin them and cut in thick slices. Heat the oil until very hot, then add the seeds. Stir around for a moment, until they start to jump around, then add the scallions. Lower the heat slightly and cook for 2 minutes, then add the chilies. Cook for another 1–2 minutes.

2 Then put in the sliced potatoes and cook together, stirring to mix well and adding sea salt and black pepper. Remove from the heat, add the yogurt and half the fresh cilantro leaves, and fold in gently. Turn into a dish to serve, scattered with the remaining cilantro leaves. Serve at room temperature or chilled.

Serves 4

1 lb. firm waxy potatoes

2 tablespoons sunflower oil

1 teaspoon black onion seeds, black mustard seeds, or poppy seeds

1 teaspoon cumin seeds

1 bunch scallions, bulbs only, thinly sliced

2 small red chilies, deseeded and finely chopped

1¼ cups yogurt

2 tablespoons cilantro leaves

sea salt and black pepper

potato cakes with cumin

1 Boil the potatoes, then drain well and skin them. Push them through a medium food mill and return to a clean pan. Dry out over gentle heat, then set aside.

2 Heat half the oil in a skillet and cook the scallions for 3 minutes, adding the cumin halfway through. Pour onto the potato purée and mix well, adding the chopped cilantro leaves, and sea salt and black pepper to taste. Chill for 1 hour to firm, if convenient, then form into small round cakes, shaping them on a floured board. Mix the ground spice with the breadcrumbs or sifted flour. Dip the cakes first in the beaten egg, then in the breadcrumbs or flour. Heat the remaining oil in a wide skillet and cook the cakes until golden on each side, about 6 minutes in all. Drain them briefly on paper towels, then serve with Fresh Tomato Sauce (see page 185), Salsa Fresca (see page 191) or tomato ketchup.

Note: If rushed, simply coat the cakes in flour and omit the egg and breadcrumbs.

Makes 8; serves 4.

1½ lb. floury potatoes

3 tablespoons sunflower oil

1 bunch scallions, sliced

2 teaspoons ground cumin

2 tablespoons chopped cilantro leaves

1 teaspoon ground turmeric, powdered saffron, or mild curry powder

8 tablespoons dry white breadcrumbs or sifted flour

1 egg, beaten

sea salt and black pepper

spring rolls
with ginger sauce

These are not worth making on a small scale, so I usually make twice the quantity and freeze half. Sprouting seeds can be bought in health food stores or made at home. See Crab Rolls with Tamarind Sauce (page 100) for advice on buying filo pastry.

1 Trim the scallions down to 1½ inches and cut them lengthwise into thin slivers. Heat a wok or deep skillet, then add the oil and reheat. Put in the scallions and stir-fry for 1 minute, then add the garlic, chilies, and ginger, and toss for another 30 seconds. Add the sprouts and stir-fry for 2 minutes, adding the pine nuts halfway through. Now add the soy sauce, sesame and chili oils, and toss for another 30 seconds. Then remove from the heat and leave to cool.

2 Unfold the filo pastry and lay 1 sheet out flat; cover the rest with a damp cloth. Cut the sheet into strips 3 x 10 inches. Brush with melted butter, then lay a heaped teaspoon of the filling in the center of the narrow end. Fold over the sides to enclose the filling, then roll up and seal the edges by brushing with more melted butter. Lay the rolls on a greased cookie sheet and repeat the process until all the filling has been used. Store in the refrigerator (or the freezer) until ready to bake, then brush with more melted butter and bake in a preheated oven, 375°F, for about 12 minutes or until golden brown.

3 While they are baking, make the ginger sauce by mixing all the ingredients together in a small pitcher or bowl. Pour into small individual dishes to serve.

Makes about 36. Half the spring rolls and all the sauce will serve 4 as a first course; the remaining spring rolls may be frozen for a future occasion.

2 bunches scallions

2 tablespoons sunflower oil

1 large garlic clove, finely chopped

12 fresh chilies, deseeded and finely chopped

1 tablespoon grated fresh root ginger

3 cups sprouts, such as lentils, mung beans, alfalfa

3 tablespoons pine nuts

1 tablespoon soy sauce

a dash of sesame oil

a dash of chili oil

about 8 oz. filo pastry

3 tablespoons butter, melted

Ginger Sauce:

3 tablespoons *sake* or dry vermouth

3 tablespoons soy sauce

2 x ½ inch squares fresh root ginger, crushed in a garlic press

polenta
with peppers and cheese soufflé sauce

1 Heat 2½ cups of lightly salted water in a pan with a heavy base. As it approaches boiling point, start to shake in the polenta gradually, stirring all the time. When it starts to boil, lower the heat and simmer gently for 5 minutes, stirring often, until it becomes thick and smooth and comes away from the sides of the pan. Then tip it out onto a wet surface, form into a cake about ½–¾ inch thick and leave to cool for 1–2 hours, or even overnight.

2 Later, using a round biscuit cutter or a cup as a guide, cut 4 circles of polenta about 2½ inches wide. Broil the peppers until their skins have blistered and blackened evenly all over, turning at regular intervals.

3 Let them cool, then scrape away the skin and discard all the seeds and interior pith. Cut each pepper into quarters.

4 Broil the polenta rounds on a hot, ridged cast-iron broiler pan on top of the heat until they are nicely marked with brown stripes. Lay them on an oiled cookie sheet and put 1 red and 1 yellow pepper quarter on each.

5 Then make the sauce: in a small pan, melt the butter, stir in the flour and cook for 1 minute. Then pour in the heated milk and cook for 3 minutes, stirring often. Stir in the mustard powder, then the grated cheese, stirring hard until all of it has melted smoothly. Lastly, stir in the sea salt and black pepper to taste, and remove from the heat.

6 Beat the egg yolks and stir into the sauce. Then whip the egg whites until stiff and fold into the sauce after it has cooled for a few moments. Pour the sauce over the polenta and pepper rounds and bake in a preheated oven, 400°F, for 15 minutes, until risen and brown. Serve immediately.

Note: If you are unable to get quick polenta, make as above but allow 40 minutes initial cooking instead of 5.

Serves 4 as a first course or as a light main dish with a green salad.

⅞ cup quick or instant polenta
1 red pepper
1 yellow pepper

Cheese soufflé sauce:
2 tablespoons butter
⅝ cup cake flour
⅝ cup milk, heated
½ teaspoon mustard powder
**⅓ cup freshly grated Parmesan or
   Gruyère cheese**
2 eggs, separated
sea salt and black pepper

fusilli
with spinach, garlic, and chili

1 Wash the spinach well, removing any tough stalks. Place it in a large pan of lightly salted boiling water. Bring back to a boil and cook, uncovered, for 4–5 minutes, depending on whether it is tender summer spinach or the tougher winter spinach. Drain and slice across into 3 inch sections.

2 Heat the oil in a wide pan and add the chopped garlic and hot red pepper flakes. Cook gently for 1–2 minutes, then add the spinach and reheat, stirring well to mix with the flavorings. Keep it warm while you cook the fusilli in plenty of lightly salted fast-boiling water. When the pasta is tender, drain it well and add to the spinach. Reheat quickly, stirring to mix, then serve immediately.

Serves 4

12 oz. spinach
4 tablespoons virgin olive oil
1 garlic clove, finely chopped
½ teaspoon hot red pepper flakes
12 oz. fusilli

potato gratin with nutmeg

This version of Gratin Dauphinois is generously flavored with nutmeg and a little garlic. Grated cheese is not included.

1 It is important that the potato slices are of an equal thickness. Butter a wide earthenware dish and make a layer of potato slices, using the uneven shaped slices in this layer, which will be hidden. Sprinkle generously with nutmeg, and with crushed garlic, sea salt, and black pepper. Continue making layers of potato and seasoning as above until all the potatoes have been used.

2 Mix the egg, cream, and milk together, adding more salt and pepper, and pour over the potatoes. There should be enough to come almost level with the top layer. Bake in a preheated oven, 350°F, for 1½ hours, until nicely browned on top. This is the best possible accompaniment to roast lamb or chicken.

Serves 4 to 6

1½ lb. waxy potatoes, peeled and
  thinly sliced
1 tablespoon butter
⅛ whole nutmeg, grated
1 large garlic clove, crushed
1 egg, beaten
1¼ cups light cream
1¼ cups milk
sea salt and black pepper

sauces

To make a simple yogurt sauce, put ¼ teaspoon lightly packed saffron stamens and ¼ teaspoon garam masala in a large metal spoon and toast them gently for 1 minute over low heat. Then pound them in a mortar and add 1 tablespoon almost-boiling water. Pound for a moment or two longer, then leave for 10 minutes to infuse. Pour onto 1¼ cups yogurt and mix lightly. This is best left for some hours before eating. Sprinkle with paprika and serve. This is good with hard-boiled eggs and cold rice dishes.

bread sauce

This is the traditional sauce to accompany roast poultry or game. The practice of sticking the cloves in the onion is a practical one; they are easy to remove after the cooking.

2 cloves
½ onion
1½ cups milk
½ bay leaf
a pinch of mace or nutmeg
about 6 tablespoons soft white breadcrumbs
1 tablespoon butter
2 tablespoons cream
sea salt and black pepper

1 Stick the cloves in the onion. Put the milk in a pan with the onion, bay leaf, mace or nutmeg, salt and pepper. Bring it very slowly to a boil, remove from the heat, cover the pan and let stand for 20–30 minutes.

2 Strain, discarding the flavorings, and reheat. As the milk nears boiling point shake in the breadcrumbs gradually, stirring all the time, and stopping as the sauce nears the right consistency; it will go on thickening slightly as it cools. Simmer gently for 3 minutes, stirring, adding salt and pepper as required. Just before serving, stir in the butter and cream, and pour into a sauceboat. Serve soon after making or it will solidify.

Serves 4

hot chili sauce

In terms of heat, this comes halfway between the Tomato Chili Sauce (see page 184) and Hot Sauces I and II (see page 185). It is a useful accompaniment for dishes such as Chinese Duck Pancakes (see page 128), or for sparking up a bland dish.

3 dried chilies, split and deseeded
1 tablespoon finely chopped onion
1 garlic clove, finely chopped
1 tablespoon olive oil
¾ cup *Passato di Pomodoro* (see page 190) or commercial passata

1 Soak the dried chilies in 4 tablespoons boiling water for 10 minutes; then drain them, reserving the water, and chop. Put the chilies in a small mill with half the soaking water and process to a purée. Set aside.

2 Cook the onion in the oil for 3 minutes, then add the garlic for 1 minute. When all is softened and lightly colored, stir in the chili purée and cook for 1 minute. Lastly, add the *Passato* and cook gently for 5 minutes. Set aside to cool. Serve at room temperature. Add sparingly, for it can be very hot indeed.

Makes ⅝ cup; serves 6.

chili mayonnaise I and II

These are excellent accompaniments to simple foods such as grilled shellfish, boiled cod, and hard-boiled eggs.

1 Put the dried chilies in a small strainer and set over a pan of boiling water. Cover the strainer and steam the chilies for 4 minutes, then remove from the pan and allow to cool. Then chop them and purée with 2 tablespoons of the olive oil in a small blender or coffee mill.

2 Put the eggs yolks in a bowl. Add the mustard powder and salt, then start adding the rest of the oil drop by drop, beating continuously with a hand-held electric beater or a whisk. When about one-third of the oil has been used, start adding the rest slightly more quickly, in a very thin stream, stopping now and then until all of it has been absorbed. You may add some of the lemon juice halfway through, if required, to thin it slightly. When all the oil has been absorbed, stir in the chili purée. Then add the rest of the lemon juice and vinegar, tasting as you do so. The blandness of the oil balances the fiery chilies perfectly, so the sauce is not too hot. If a hotter sauce is required, simply increase the number of chilies.

Makes 1¼ cups; serves 4.

Version I:

2 dried chilies, deseeded and stalks removed
1¼ cups light olive oil
2 egg yolks
a pinch of mustard powder
a pinch of sea salt
1½ tablespoons lemon juice
1½ tablespoons white wine vinegar

Make the mayonnaise as above, but omit the dried chili purée. Put the chili powder in a large metal spoon and hold it over a gentle heat for a few seconds, moving it about and being careful not to let it change color. (If it burns, it will taste bitter and ruin the sauce.) Add it gradually to the mayonnaise, stirring it in well and tasting as you do so. Stop when the degree of spicy heat you desire is reached.

Makes 1¼ cups; serves 4.

Version II

1¼ cups mayonnaise, made as above
1–2 teaspoons chili powder

ginger salsa

The addition of grated fresh ginger to a salsa is certainly not authentic, but it is very delicious and seems curiously appropriate. This easy, fresh-tasting, light sauce is excellent with fried food of all kinds, particularly fish, shellfish, chicken, croquettes, and fish cakes.

1 Put the dried chilies in a small bowl and pour 4 tablespoons boiling water over them. Stand for 20 minutes, then lift out the chilies and chop them coarsely. Purée them in a small blender or coffee mill with half their soaking liquid.

2 Put the chopped tomatoes in a food processor with the puréed chilies, chopped scallions, grated ginger, chopped cilantro leaves, lime juice, sea salt, and black pepper. Process briefly; it does not need to be a smooth purée. Serve chilled or at room temperature.

Serves 4

- 2 dried chilies, halved and deseeded
- 2 large ripe tomatoes, skinned and coarsely chopped
- 4 scallions, bulbs only, chopped
- 2 teaspoons grated fresh root ginger
- 2 tablespoons chopped fresh cilantro leaves
- 1 tablespoon lime juice
- sea salt and black pepper

tomato chili sauce

A well-made tomato sauce, light but spicy, is a welcome relief from all the ersatz ones in jars and cans. Quickly made, it can be kept for 2–3 days in the refrigerator or be stored in the freezer. The degree of heat can be varied, according to the dish it is to accompany. It goes well with a wide range of foods, including pasta, gnocchi, egg or chicken croquettes, broiled shellfish, and fried chicken.

1 Cook the chopped shallot in the butter and oil over a moderate heat for 3–4 minutes. Then add the finely chopped garlic, chili(es) and ginger, and continue to cook, stirring often, for another 3 minutes.

2 Put in the tomatoes, adding the sugar and thyme, sea salt and black pepper, and simmer for 15–20 minutes, until well softened. Then remove from the heat and stir in the basil.

Serves 4

- 1 shallot, finely chopped
- 2 tablespoons butter
- 2 tablespoons olive oil
- 1 garlic clove, finely chopped
- 1–2 red chilies, deseeded and finely chopped
- ¾ inch square fresh root ginger, peeled and finely chopped
- 4 large tomatoes, skinned and chopped
- ½ teaspoon sugar
- ½ teaspoon thyme
- 1 tablespoon basil, cut in thin strips
- sea salt and black pepper

hot sauce I and II

The first Hot Sauce is made with Harissa (see page 59), the ultra-hot paste based on chili peppers and used throughout the Arab countries of North Africa. It can be made at home or bought fairly easily in tubes and small cans.

Version I:

½ teaspoon Harissa (see page 59)

I tablespoon tomato purée

2 tablespoons hot chicken, meat, fish, or vegetable stock

Mix the harissa with the tomato purée in a small bowl. Stir in the hot stock, which should be taken from the dish it is to accompany — usually a lamb, chicken, or vegetable stew made to serve with couscous. Pour into a tiny dish and serve with the couscous.

Serves 4 to 6

Version II

I teaspoon ground cumin

I teaspoon ground coriander

½ teaspoon chili powder

2 tablespoons tomato purée

2 tablespoons hot chicken, meat, fish, or vegetable stock

This is a quick and easy substitute for the real thing, to be made when you do not have any harissa, nor the inclination to make some.

Mix the spices and stir them into the tomato purée. Add the hot stock, taken from the dish the sauce is to accompany, and pour into a small bowl, to serve with the couscous.

Serves 4 to 6

fresh tomato sauce

The degree of heat in this sauce can be adjusted by reducing the amount of chilies, or even leaving them out altogether, depending on the dish the sauce is to accompany. A dish that is already hot does not want a fiery accompaniment.

I lb. tomatoes, skinned and cut in quarters

½ bunch scallions, bulbs only, sliced

I tablespoon sunflower oil

2 small chilies, red or green, deseeded and finely chopped

Put the tomatoes in a food processor and process until reduced to a chunky purée. Cook the sliced scallions in the oil for 2 minutes, then add the chopped chilies and cook for 2 minutes more. Add to the tomatoes in the food processor and process again, briefly, until reduced to a fairly coarse purée. If serving warm, pour into a small pan and heat gently. Serve warm at room temperature, or chilled.

Makes about 1³/₄ cups

saffron sauce

This sauce needs to be made with powdered saffron rather than with threads.

1 Put the egg yolk into a bowl and stir in the saffron, cumin, and coriander. Add the oil drop by drop, beating with a wooden spoon until each addition has been absorbed. When half has been incorporated, the oil can be added more quickly.
2 When all the oil has been used, stir in the vinegar and lemon juice. Lastly, fold in the yogurt and turn into a clean bowl. Serve cold with hot broiled or poached fish.

Serves 4

1 egg yolk
¼ teaspoon powdered saffron
¼ teaspoon ground cumin
¼ teaspoon ground coriander
⅝ cup sunflower oil
½ tablespoon white wine vinegar
½ tablespoon lemon juice
⅝ cup yogurt

smoky salsa

This tasty sauce complements all manner of bland foods, such as shellfish, fish cakes, egg croquettes, and vegetable fritters.

1–2 smoked dried chilies, halved and
   deseeded
10 oz. tomatoes
1 red pepper
1 bunch scallions, sliced
2 tablespoons lime juice
2 tablespoons chopped
   cilantro leaves
sea salt and black pepper

1 Put the dried chili(es) in a small bowl and cover with 4 tablespoons boiling water; leave for 20 minutes, then process in small blender or coffee mill with half the soaking water. Stick the tomatoes and the pepper on skewers and broil them, turning frequently. The tomatoes will take just a few minutes, the pepper slightly longer. When the skins have charred evenly all over, remove them from the broiler and leave to cool. Then remove the skins, discard the seeds from the pepper, and cut both vegetables into chunks.

2 Put vegetables into a food processor with the scallions, chili purée, sea salt, and black pepper. Process until blended into a lumpy purée; pour into a bowl and stir in the lime juice and chopped cilantro leaves. Serve cold or at room temperature.

Makes 1¼ cups; serves 6.

hot mustard sauce

1 Melt the butter, add the flour and cook for 1 minute, stirring. Then pour in the heated stock and bring to a boil, stirring until blended. Simmer for 3 minutes, then add the mustard, beating it in with a wire whisk until smooth. Add sea salt and black pepper, then put in the *crème fraîche* or sour cream in dollops, stirring to blend smoothly.

2 Reheat gently — don't allow it to boil again — then stir in the chopped dill, reserving a little as a garnish. Pour the sauce into a heated sauceboat and sprinkle the rest of the dill on top. Serve with boiled lobster, prawns, poached white fish, or salmon. If serving with poached or broiled chicken, hard-boiled eggs, or vegetables, use chicken stock instead of fish stock.

Serves 4

3 tablespoons butter
2 tablespoons all-purpose flour
1¼ cups fish or chicken stock, heated
1 tablespoon Dijon mustard
1¼ cups *crème fraîche* or sour cream
2 tablespoons chopped dill weed
sea salt and black pepper

cold mustard sauce

This is a useful picnic sauce, as it goes with so many different foods.

1 Lower the egg into lightly salted boiling water and cook for exactly 5 minutes. Cool briefly, then shell it and cut it in half, holding it over a bowl. Let the runny yolk fall into the bowl; discard the white. Stir the mustard into the yolk, then, very slowly, start adding the oil drop by drop, exactly as if making mayonnaise, beating all the time with a wooden spoon.

2 When all the oil has been absorbed, fold in the yogurt and, lastly, the lemon juice. Salt and pepper will not be needed. Serve cold with warm boiled or steamed vegetables, such as new potatoes in their skins, asparagus, broccoli, or cauliflower; with shellfish; warm grilled chicken wings; or with Spiced Meatballs (see page 144).

Makes 1¼ cups; serves 4.

1 egg
½ tablespoon Dijon mustard
5 tablespoons sunflower oil
⅝ cup yogurt
½ tablespoon lemon juice, or to taste

quick mustard sauce

Here is a sauce to make in a hurry, using commercial mayonnaise unless you have already made some yourself.

1 Put all the ingredients except the lemon juice and chopped herb in a blender or food processor. Process until blended, then add the lemon juice, blending by hand and tasting as you do so.

2 Pour into a bowl and scatter the finely chopped herb, if using, over the top. Serve with hard-boiled eggs, boiled or steamed vegetable, or cold chicken.

Makes just over 1¼ cups; serves 4 to 6.

⅝ **cup mayonnaise**
⅝ **cup yogurt**
1 **tablespoon Dijon mustard**
2 **tablespoons lemon juice,**
or to taste
1 **tablespoon finely chopped dill**
weed or chervil, to garnish
(optional)

Romesco sauce

This fiery sauce from Catalonia is traditionally served with boiled or grilled shellfish, either hot or cold. It may also be served in conjunction with a mayonnaise and mixed to taste by each person. In Catalonia it can be found in tapas bars and in restaurants, as well as in the home.

1 Soak the chili in boiling water for 10 minutes, then drain and chop. Toast the almonds gently in a dry skillet, turning over with a spatula until they are light golden or straw-colored. Then pour them out and put the pine nuts into the same pan and repeat the process. Be sure to pour them out once the right color has been reached, for they will continue to cook in the heat of the pan.

2 Put both nuts in the food processor with the chopped chili and garlic. Process until blended, then add the chopped tomato and process again, adding the oil and vinegar through the lid of the processor. Season to taste with some sea salt and black pepper.

Makes about 1 cup, but serves 6, as it is very strong.

1 **dried red chili, halved and**
deseeded
¼ **cup whole blanched almonds**
2 **tablespoons pine nuts**
2 **garlic cloves, finely chopped**
1 **large tomato, chopped**
⅝ **cup olive oil**
2 **tablespoons red or white wine**
vinegar
sea salt and black pepper

sahaaweq

1–2 green chilies, split and seeded

3 cloves garlic, peeled

2 oz. hard, salty white cheese, such as
 feta

3 small tomatoes, unpeeled, cut into
 chunks

¼ oz. fresh cilantro leaves

⅛ oz. fresh mint

¼ teaspoon sea salt

¼ teaspoon ground cumin

5 cardamom pods, seeds only, ground

1 teaspoon dried wild thyme, or
 summer savory

In Sana'a, the capital of Yemen, each day at about noon primitive sorts of juice bars spring up on the street corners. These consist of old-fashioned kitchen grinders clamped to wooden crates, with little bowls of green chilies, garlic cloves, a smoky local cheese not unlike feta, tomatoes, cumin, wild thyme, salt, and bunches of fresh cilantro and mint. These are pushed through the grinder, and the resulting purée — bright green and juicy — is caught in small plastic bags and sold off to the customers, who take it to the nearby café, and eat it with hot Arab (pita) bread. I use it as any other salsa: served raw, over pasta, lentils, or sliced raw vegetables. It is a delicious sauce, pungent and healthy, but so stimulating that it tends to keep one awake at night, like drinking too much black coffee.

Push all the ingredients through an old-fashioned grinder, or chop in a food processor until reduced to a chunky purée. Serve cold.

Makes ¾ cup

passato di pomodoro

2 lb. tomatoes, unskinned, cut in
 quarters

½ teaspoon sugar (optional)

1 Put the quartered tomatoes in a heavy, broad-based pan and place it over a gentle heat. Simmer very slowly for about 1 hour, stirring now and then, adding 2 tablespoons boiling water from time to time to prevent sticking. When the contents of the pan have been reduced to a thick purée, taste, and add the sugar if necessary.

2 Remove the pan from the heat and push the purée through a coarse strainer or medium food mill. (Do not use a food processor, because the skins and seeds need to be held back.) Spoon the purée into jars and leave to cool, then close the jars tightly and store them in the refrigerator.

Note: A quick, hot sauce can be made by stirring ½ teaspoon harissa (see page 59) into 2 tablespoons *passato di pomodoro*. This makes a delicious sandwich spread on buttered rye bread and topped with sliced mozzarella cheese, sprinkled with some freshly milled black pepper.

Makes about 1⅛ cups

salsa fresca

This quickly made version of the famous Southwestern sauce makes a delicious side dish to serve with curries.

If the tomatoes are not perfectly ripe, it may be better to skin them before chopping. Put all the ingredients in a food processor and blend briefly; the salsa should not be smooth. Serve chilled or at room temperature with hot or cold curries. **Note:** When serving with a hot curry, you may prefer to use only a ½ chili, or even omit it altogether. With bland dishes, on the other hand, you can use 2 chilies.

Serves 4

10 oz. ripe tomatoes, unskinned and
   roughly chopped
4 scallions, cut in chunks
1 red or green chili, deseeded and
   finely chopped
1 tablespoon lime juice
2 tablespoons roughly chopped
   cilantro leaves

rouille

This pungent Provençal sauce is the essential accompaniment to Mediterranean fish soups, made with a mixture of fish and spiced with saffron, orange rind, and fennel. The basic ingredients of saffron, garlic, and chilies may be thickened with soaked bread or mashed potato, enriched with egg yolk, pounded in a mortar or puréed in a food processor. The resulting purée may be spread on small slices of French bread that have been dried in a low oven and floated in the soup, or may be simply stirred into the hot soup.

1 Soak the bread in the stock, soup, or milk for 5 minutes, then squeeze dry. Pound the chilies, garlic, salt, and saffron in a mortar; add the egg yolk, if using, and pound again. Add the soaked bread and pound until blended to a paste. Add the oil drop by drop, stirring with a spoon, as if making mayonnaise.

2 When all is blended, stir in 1 tablespoon of the fish soup to thin the rouille slightly. Place in a small bowl and serve with fish soup, accompanied by slices of French bread.

Note: I usually add an egg yolk, as this makes the sauce more smooth, as well as slightly more robust and less likely to separate. If you prefer, you may make the sauce without the egg yolk, reserving it for use in an emergency. Then, if your sauce does separate, start again by breaking an egg yolk into a clean bowl and stirring the split sauce into it very slowly.

Serves 6

⅓ oz. dry white bread
3 tablespoons fish stock, fish soup,
   or milk
2 dried chilies, deseeded and finely
   chopped
2 garlic cloves, finely chopped
½ teaspoon sea salt
¼ teaspoon saffron threads
1 egg yolk (optional)
3 tablespoons extra virgin olive oil
1 tablespoon fish soup

lemon sauce

1 Mix the sugar and corn flour (available in health food stores; it has the flavor of corn meal, but is more finely milled) in a bowl. Heat 1¼ cups water to boiling point, then pour it slowly onto the sugar and corn flour, stirring constantly. Pour the mixture into a pan and reheat slowly, stirring constantly, without allowing it to reach a full boil. Simmer gently for 5 minutes, then remove from the heat. Stir in little pieces of butter, waiting until each batch has melted before adding more. Then add the lemon juice and grated rind. Serve warm with baked or steamed sponge cakes or puddings.

Serves 4

¼ cup vanilla sugar or granulated sugar
1 tablespoon corn flour
¼ cup butter, cut in small pieces
juice (about 2½ tablespoons) and grated rind of 1 (preferably unwaxed) lemon

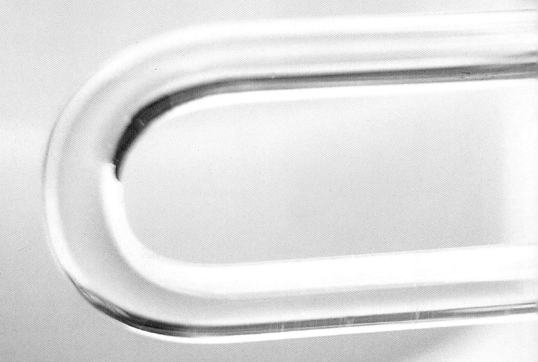

blood orange sauce

2 tablespoons vanilla sugar or granulated sugar
1 tablespoon corn flour
¼ cup butter, cut in small pieces
juice (6–8 tablespoons) and grated
   rind of 1½ blood oranges

This beautiful rosy red sauce looks pretty served warm over Vanilla Ice Cream (see page 243). It is also good served with a plain steamed pudding or a marmalade sponge cake. When blood oranges are not available, ordinary oranges can be used, but the sauce will not be as pretty.

1 Mix the sugar and corn flour in a bowl. Heat 1¼ cups water to boiling point, then pour it slowly onto the sugar and corn flour, stirring constantly. Pour the mixture into a pan and reheat slowly, stirring all the time. Simmer gently for 5 minutes; remove from the heat. Stir in little pieces of butter, waiting until each batch has melted before adding more. Then add the orange juice and grated rind.

Serves 4 to 6

yogurt sauce

Although not a spice recipe as such, this bland and cooling sauce is the perfect foil for fiery foods such as chili-based dishes.

⅝ cup yogurt
2 tomatoes, skinned and chopped
¼ cucumber, peeled and chopped
sea salt and black pepper

Put the yogurt in a bowl and beat until smooth. Add the tomatoes, cucumber, salt, and pepper. Mix gently, turn into a bowl. Serve chilled or at room temperature.
Note: If preferred, the tomatoes may be omitted and twice as much cucumber used, unpeeled and coarsely grated. In this case, be sure to squeeze excess moisture out of the cucumbers before adding them to the yogurt.

Serves 4

ginger sauce

This is a very delicious sauce for serving with baked or steamed sponge cake, apple puddings, or Vanilla Ice Cream (see page 243). The preserved ginger is not essential, but it adds a subtle and complex flavor to the sauce.

1⅛ cups milk
½ vanilla pod, split
3 egg yolks
2½ tablespoons vanilla sugar or granulated sugar
½ tablespoon ground ginger
2 teaspoons syrup from jar of preserved stem ginger (optional)
1½–2 tablespoons finely chopped preserved stem ginger (optional)

1 Put the milk in a pan. Scrape the seeds from the vanilla pod into the milk, also adding the pod. Warm the milk slowly; when about to boil, turn off the heat and cover. Leave for 30 minutes to infuse, then reheat gently and remove the pod.
2 Put the egg yolks in a large bowl, add the sugar and ground ginger, and start beating with a hand-held electric beater or a balloon whisk. When the milk is about to boil for the second time, pour it onto the egg yolks, continuing to beat. Stand the bowl over a saucepan half full of simmering water and stir briskly with a wooden spoon until the sauce starts to thicken. This may take as long as 8 minutes. When it has thickened enough to coat the back of the spoon, remove the bowl from the pan and stand it in a sink half full of cold water. Stir occasionally as it cools to prevent a skin from forming. If you have some preserved stem ginger, add the syrup and finely chopped pieces to the finished sauce. Then process briefly in a blender or food processor. Serve warm with hot or cold puddings, or ice cream.

Serves 4 to 6

vanilla custard sauce

This delicious sweet sauce is not to be confused with commercial preparations. It is the best possible accompaniment to fruit or steamed puddings.

1 Put the milk in a small pan. Scrape the seeds out of the vanilla pod into the milk, adding the pod itself. Warm the milk slowly; when it is about to boil, turn off the heat and cover the pan. Leave for 30 minutes to infuse, then reheat gently and remove the pod.

2 Put the egg yolks in a large bowl, add the sugar, and start beating with a hand-held electric beater or a balloon whisk. When the milk is about to boil for the second time, pour it onto the egg yolks, continuing to beat. Stand the bowl over a saucepan half full of simmering water and stir briskly with a wooden spoon until the sauce starts to thicken. This may take as long as 8 minutes. When it has thickened enough to coat the back of the spoon, remove the bowl from the pan and stand it in a sink half full of cold water. Stir every now and then as it cools to prevent a skin from forming. Serve warm or at room temperature.

Note: For a richer, more luxurious sauce, use only 1¼ cups of milk and fold in ⅝ cup whipped heavy cream at the very end, after cooling.

Serves 4 to 6

1⅞ **cups milk**
½ **vanilla pod**
3 egg yolks
2½ **tablespoons vanilla sugar or granulated sugar**

breads, cakes, and cookies

For a sustaining snack, toast some sesame seeds in a dry skillet for 2–3 minutes over gentle heat, until they start to color and jump around; then scatter over thick slices of brown bread and butter. This is also delicious shaken over salads, cooked vegetables, and hard-boiled eggs.

celery seed bread

Seed breads are both unusual and delicious, and can be varied to suit different foods by the choice of seed. My current favorite is made with celery seeds, for eating with cheese and with vegetable dishes. Aniseed or caraway seeds may be substituted for the celery seeds.

1 Put the flour in a large bowl with the salt. Crumble the fresh yeast into a small bowl, or shake in the dried yeast, and add the sugar. Heat the milk to lukewarm and add 2 tablespoons of it to the yeast. If using fresh yeast, let it stand in a warm place for 10 minutes before using. In another small bowl mix the egg with the seeds. Make a well in the center of the flour. Mix the yeast with the egg and pour into the well. Cover with some of the flour and yeast and pour most of the remaining milk over it, reserving a little. Beat hard with a wooden spoon to mix, until the dough starts to cling together. Add a little more milk if required. Then turn the dough out onto a floured surface and knead hard for 6–8 minutes, or until smooth and elastic. Clean the bowl, rub with oil, and replace the dough. Cover with plastic wrap and then leave to stand in a warm place for 1–1½ hours, or until doubled in volume.

2 Oil a loaf pan holding roughly 3 pints. Punch down the dough, turn out, and knead again for 5 minutes. Form into a loaf shape and put in the pan. Cover with a towel and put back in a warm place to rise again for about 45 minutes, or until the dough is level with the top of the pan.

3 Bake the loaf in a preheated oven, 400°F, for 40 minutes, or until it sounds hollow when tapped on the bottom. Turn out onto a wire rack to cool.

Note: Celery-seed bread is absolutely delicious with cheese of all kinds, especially hard cheese such as manchego and brebis, soft cream cheeses, and goat cheese. It is also good with minestrone-type soups, and with oily Provençal dishes such as ratatouille. Caraway-seed bread is also very good with cheese, while aniseed bread goes well with fish soups such as bouillabaisse. All the seed breads are good toasted or used for making croûtons or breadcrumbs.

Makes a 1½ lb. loaf

4¼ cups bread flour
½ teaspoon sea salt
½ oz. fresh yeast or 1 tablespoon
   dried yeast
1 tablespoon sugar
1⅛ cups milk
1 egg, beaten
1½ tablespoons celery (or other)
   seeds

saffron bread

This is a medieval dish, but as delicious, and as adaptable, today as it ever was. It is excellent served with a fish terrine, or with Mediterranean dishes such as fish soup, minestrone, soupe au pistou, and oily vegetable dishes such as ratatouille and piperade. It is also good broiled on a cast-iron broiler pan on top of the heat and treated like bruschetta, or toasted and used as a base for egg dishes. When stale, it makes superb croûtons for serving with fish soup, or breadcrumbs for coating fish or fish cakes before frying. It also freezes well.

4½ cups bread flour

½ tablespoon sea salt

½ oz. fresh yeast or 1 tablespoon dried yeast

½ teaspoon saffron threads

⅝ cup milk, heated

2 eggs, beaten

1 Put the flour and salt in a large bowl. Crumble the fresh yeast into a small bowl, or shake in the dried yeast, and add 4 tablespoons lukewarm water. If using fresh yeast, let stand in a warm place for 10 minutes before using. Toast the saffron threads gently in a dry skillet for 10–15 seconds, then pound in a mortar. Pour the heated milk over the saffron and leave to steep for about 10 minutes. Then pour the saffron-flavored milk onto the beaten eggs and mix well.

2 Make a well in the center of the flour and pour in the yeast mixture. Cover it with some of the flour, then pour in the saffron and egg mixture. Beat hard with a wooden spoon. If the mixture seems too dry, add a very little more milk or water. Once it starts to cling together, turn out onto a floured surface and knead for 5–6 minutes. Clean the bowl, rub with oil and replace the dough. Cover with plastic wrap and stand in a warm place for 1–1½ hours or until doubled in volume.

3 Grease a loaf pan holding roughly 3 pints or 2 loaf pans holding roughly 1 pint each. Punch down the dough, turn out and knead for another 5 minutes. Then form into 1–2 loaves and put into the pan(s). Cover with a towel and put back in a warm place for another 45–60 minutes for the large loaf, 20–25 minutes for the small loaves, or until the dough has filled the pans.

4 Bake the large loaf in a preheated oven, 375°F, for 30–40 minutes and the small loaves for 20–25 minutes, or until the bread sounds hollow when tapped on the bottom. Turn out on to a wire rack to cool.

Makes 1 x 1 lb. loaf or 2 x 8 oz. loaves

This is James Beard's classic recipe for cornbread, with chilies added. These need not be smoked chilies; plain dried or fresh chilies will do perfectly well.

**1 smoked chili, halved and
   deseeded
⅔ cup cake flour
3 teaspoons baking powder
1⅛ cups fine polenta
1 teaspoon sugar
1 teaspoon sea salt
3 eggs, beaten
1¼ cups milk
¼ cup butter, melted
2 tablespoons chopped
   cilantro leaves (optional)**

1 Butter a square baking pan measuring about 8 inches wide by 1½ inches deep, or a small loaf pan measuring 8 x 3 x 3 inches.

2 Put the smoked chili in a small bowl and cover with 4 tablespoons boiling water. Leave for 20 minutes, then lift out the chili and chop. Sift the flour, baking powder, polenta, and sugar into a large bowl. Using your fingers, crumble in the sea salt, if it is soft enough, or lightly crush it in a mortar first.

3 Mix the beaten eggs with the milk. Make a well in the center of the dry ingredients and start to pour in the liquid mixture, beating all the time with a wooden spoon and incorporating the dry ingredients from around the edge to make a smooth batter. Then stir in the melted butter.

4 Finally, stir in the chopped chili and the cilantro leaves, if using. Pour the mixture into the baking pan and bake in a preheated oven, 400°F. The square pan should bake for 15–20 minutes or the loaf pan for 40 minutes.

Serves 6

cornbread with smoked chilies

spiced raisin bread

A word of warning: unless you have a mixer — not a food processor or blender — this is quite messy and troublesome to make, but the results are excellent and worth the trouble. It is delicious sliced and spread with butter, halfway between a bread and a cake. It keeps well wrapped in foil and stored in a container, and is an invaluable stand-by over a holiday. While you are making it, you may prefer to double the quantities and freeze 1 loaf.

4½ cups bread flour

½ teaspoon sea salt

½ oz. fresh yeast or 1 tablespoon dried yeast

3 tablespoons butter, cut in small pieces

1 egg, beaten

5 tablespoons milk, warmed

½ cup raisins

1 cup mixed dried fruit

⅓ cup light brown sugar

½ tablespoon molasses

½ teaspoon mixed spice *or* ground nutmeg, cinnamon, and cloves, mixed

1 Put the flour and salt in a large bowl and stand in a warm place covered with a cloth. Put the yeast in a cup with 2 tablespoons warm water and let stand in a warm place for 10 minutes. Cut the butter into the flour mixture. Mix the beaten egg with the milk in a measuring cup and make up to 1 cup with warm water. Make a well in the middle of the flour and pour in the yeast, followed by the egg mixture. Stir hard to mix, adding 1–2 tablespoons water if required to make the dough cling together. Turn out on to a floured surface and knead for 3–4 minutes. Clean the bowl, rub with oil and replace the dough. Cover with a cloth and put back in a warm place to rise for 30 minutes.

2 While the dough is rising, put the raisins and other dried fruit in a bowl, also in a warm place. When the dough has risen, turn it out and knead for 5 minutes, then stir in the dried fruit, sugar, molasses, and spices. (This is the messy part.) Mix well. Once again clean the bowl, rub it with oil, and replace the dough. Cover and put back in a warm place to rise for 1½ hours.

3 Oil a loaf pan holding roughly 3 pints or 2 pans holding roughly 1½ pints each. Form the dough into 1–2 rolls and place in the pan(s). Put the pan(s) back in a warm place for another 20 minutes, covered. Bake the large loaf for 1¼ hours and the 2 small loaves for 30 minutes in a preheated oven, 350°F. Then take out of the tins and lay them on their sides on the oven rack, turn off the oven, and leave for another 5 minutes.

Makes 1 x 1¾ lb. loaf or 2 x 14 oz. loaves.

spiced fruit cake

This is an old Scottish recipe, which I like to make after Christmas, when Seville oranges or blood oranges are readily available. It makes quite a small cake; I use a loaf pan measuring roughly 9 x 4 x 2½ inches deep. The cake keeps well and is useful over a weekend or holiday, or to take on a picnic.

1 Butter a pan holding about 1¾ pints and line it with waxed paper.

2 Cream the butter with the sugar, then stir in the warm molasses and mix well. Break 1 egg into a cup and beat with a fork. Stir into the mixture, followed by a spoonful of flour. Repeat the process. When both eggs are incorporated, in a separate bowl mix the baking powder and spices with the remaining flour and then fold into the main mixture. Now stir in the ground almonds and dried fruit, then the milk and orange juice. Turn the mixture into the pan, loosely cover with a piece of foil, and bake in a preheated oven, 325°F, for 1¼ hours. Remove the foil and continue baking for another 30 minutes to allow the cake to brown. This cake keeps well wrapped in foil in a cake tin.

Makes an 1¾ lb. cake

½ cup butter

½ cup dark brown sugar

1 tablespoon molasses, warmed

2 eggs

1½ cups cake flour

½ teaspoon baking powder

1 teaspoon ground cloves

1 teaspoon ground cinnamon

1 teaspoon ground nutmeg

½ cup ground almonds

1⅓ cups mixed dried fruit

2 tablespoons milk

2 tablespoons orange juice (use Seville or blood oranges when available)

sesame breadsticks

1 Put the yeast and sugar in a cup with 3 tablespoons of tepid water. Leave in a warm place for 10 minutes. Melt the salt in 2 tablespoons very hot water, then add ⅝ cup tepid water. Put the flour in a warm bowl and make a well in the center. Pour in the yeast mixture, followed by the oil. Add just enough of the salty water to make the dough cling together, stirring until well mixed, then turn out on a floured surface and knead for 3–4 minutes, until smooth and elastic. Cover with a cloth and leave for 5 minutes.

2 Turn out again and knead once or twice, then divide the dough into 16 pieces. Roll each one out as thick as your middle finger. Lay them on oiled cookie sheets and stand them in a warm place until they start to swell, 12–15 minutes.

3 Scatter the sesame seeds on a sheet of paper, brush the breadsticks all over with beaten egg, and roll them in the seeds. Then put them back on the cookie sheets and bake in a preheated oven, 300°F, for about 35 minutes, until crisp and golden. Cool on a wire rack for about 10 minutes before serving. Alternatively, make in advance and reheat gently in a low oven, or pack into plastic bags as soon as they have cooled, and freeze.

Makes 16

¼ oz. fresh yeast
2 teaspoons sugar
1 teaspoon sea salt
2¼ cups bread flour
1 tablespoon olive oil
3–4 tablespoons sesame seeds
1 egg, beaten

cheese straws

These little pastry biscuits, highly seasoned with cheese, mustard, and cayenne, were served as a savory in days gone by. Now they make a simple canapé to serve with drinks or to accompany a consommé. The final stage, adding beaten egg white and extra Parmesan cheese, is optional; some people prefer the straws left plain.

1 cup cake flour, sifted

¼ cup butter, cut in small pieces

1 teaspoon mustard powder

½ teaspoon sea salt

¼ teaspoon cayenne

⅔ cup freshly grated Parmesan cheese

2 egg yolks, beaten

about 2 tablespoons iced water

oil for greasing

1 egg white, lightly beaten (optional)

1 Put the sifted flour in a food processor with the butter. Process, then add the mustard powder, sea salt, cayenne, and most of the grated Parmesan, reserving 1½ tablespoons for the (optional) final glaze. Process again, then add the beaten eggs through the lid while processing. Add enough iced water while processing to make a firm dough.

2 Alternatively, sift the flour into a bowl and cut in the butter by hand. Then add the grated Parmesan, mixing with the blade of a knife, and the mustard powder, salt, and cayenne. Finally, stir in the beaten egg yolks with enough iced water to make a firm dough.

3 Wrap the dough in plastic wrap and chill for 45 minutes. Roll out the dough to a thickness of ¼ inch, cut into sticks about ¼ x 3 inches and lay on oiled cookie sheets. If adding the final glaze, brush the sticks with the lightly beaten egg white and sprinkle with the reserved Parmesan. Bake in a preheated oven, 400°F, for 8–10 minutes until light golden brown.

Makes about 50

seed cake

Caraway seeds are an acquired taste, and this old-fashioned English cake will arouse strong feelings, for or against.

1 Butter a loaf pan measuring approximately 8 x 2 x 3 inches deep and line it with waxed paper.

2 Blend the butter and sugar in a food processor or by hand. Drop in through the lid, or beat in by hand, 1 egg, then 1 heaped tablespoon of flour, then the second egg and the rest of the flour. Shake in the caraway seeds and orange rind. Blend or beat thoroughly by hand. Pour the dough into the pan and bake in a preheated oven, 325°F, for 1¼ hours. Turn out and cool on a wire rack.

3 It is best to use the smaller amount of caraway seeds the first time you make this cake, and increase it to taste on subsequent occasions. Real addicts, like my daughter-in-law's father, would complain if there were too few caraway seeds that "they must have been thrown in from a great distance."

Makes a 1½ lb. cake

¾ **cup butter**
½ **cup granulated sugar**
2 eggs
2¼ **cups self-raising flour, sifted**
½–**I tablespoon caraway seeds**
grated rind of ½ **large orange**

spiced pita bread

1 Warm flat pita bread in the oven, just enough to make it easy to split in half, then cut each half across into 2 pieces, making 4 for each oval pita. (If using small round pita, simply split them in half.) Allow 1 teaspoon olive oil for each piece, smearing it across the surface. Then scatter 1 teaspoon of one of the spice mixtures across each cut surface.

2 Lay the pita pieces, seeds upward, on a cookie sheet and bake in a preheated oven, 375°F, for 5–6 minutes. Serve soon after baking if possible, while the pita are still warm, although they can be kept in an airtight container for 2–3 days and then warmed in a low oven before serving.

pita bread
olive oil

Spice mixtures:
Dukkah (see page 62)
Za'atar (see page 62)
equal parts sesame seeds and cumin seeds, roasted and ground together

sticky gingerbread

1 Put the syrup, molasses, sugar, butter, and spices in an ovenproof bowl and warm them in a preheated oven, 250°F, for 30 minutes or until the butter and sugar have melted. Then remove from the oven and turn up the heat to 375°F. Butter a large loaf pan holding 2½ pints and line it with buttered waxed paper.

2 Sift the flour with the baking soda and stir into the spiced mixture, then stir in the milk and beaten eggs. Turn the mixture into the pan and bake in the preheated oven for 1–1 ¼ hours, then take it out of the oven and leave it to cool. After about 20 minutes turn it out of the pan and lay it on a wire rack to finish cooling. Then wrap it in foil and store it in an airtight container. (It is best kept for a week before eating.) Cut in thick slices to serve, spread with unsalted butter.

Makes a 2½ lb. cake

- 1½ cups golden syrup, if available, or substitute 1 part dark corn syrup and 5 parts light corn syrup
- ½ cup dark molasses
- ⅓ cup soft brown sugar
- ¼ cup butter
- 1 tablespoon ground ginger
- 1 teaspoon mixed spice
- 2¾ cups cake flour
- ½ teaspoon baking soda
- ⅝ cup milk
- 2 eggs, beaten

cinnamon toast

This is good served with coffee or tea, midmorning or as an afternoon snack.

Mix the sugar and cinnamon in a cup. Toast the bread lightly, then spread 1 side with butter and sprinkle thickly with the sugar and cinnamon. Heat under the broiler until the sugar has melted, watching like a hawk to prevent it from burning. Cut in broad strips to serve. Serve immediately, while still hot.

Makes 12–16 pieces

- 2 tablespoons sugar
- ½ teaspoon ground cinnamon
- 4 large slices dry white bread
- butter

These are delicate, lacy cookies for serving with ices or sorbets.

1 Sift the flour with the ginger and cut in the butter. Add the sugar and cut in lightly. Warm the syrup and molasses with the cream and mix with the dry ingredients, beating with a wooden spoon. (Be very careful to level off the spoons of syrup and molasses with a knife; it is easy to use more than you mean to, in which case the cookies will not become crisp.) Alternatively, all the mixing may be done in a food processor.

2 Using 2 teaspoons, drop ½ teaspoonfuls of the mixture on to ungreased cookie sheets, leaving at least 2 inches between them. Bake in a preheated oven, 350°F, for 8–10 minutes. Remove from the oven and cool for 3–4 minutes before lifting the cookies with a palette knife. They will become crisp on cooling. They can be kept for a few days in an airtight container, or the dough may be made in advance and frozen.

Makes about 20

ginger thins

½ **cup cake flour**
½ **teaspoon ground ginger**
¼ **cup butter, cut in small pieces**
¼ **cup light brown sugar**
1 **tablespoon golden syrup, if available, or substitute 1 part dark corn syrup and 5 parts light corn syrup**
1 **tablespoon molasses**
1 **tablespoon heavy cream**

These little cookies come from Greece, where they are served as an aperitif with drinks.

1 Grease a cookie sheet. Cream the butter and sugar by hand. Add the ouzo or vodka and mix to a smooth cream. Work in the sifted flour gradually, stopping when you have a soft dough. Just mix it lightly, do not knead. Form into a sausage about 1½ inches in diameter and cut in slices about ½ inch thick.

2 Flatten each one slightly in the palm of your hand, pressing with your thumb to make a little hollow in the center of the concave side. Press a clove into each hollow, lay the cookies on the cookie sheet, and bake in a preheated oven, 300°F, for 20 minutes. They should still be quite pale, but firm and crisp. While still hot, sprinkle them with a little confectioners' sugar through a small sieve. Leave on the cookie sheet until they have cooled. Serve soon after making.

Variation: Omit the cloves and after baking sprinkle the cookies with a mixture of 2 parts confectioners' sugar to 1 part ground allspice.

Makes about 20

½ **cup butter, plus a little for greasing**
1 tablespoon granulated sugar
1 tablespoon ouzo or vodka
about 1 cup cake flour, sifted
about 20 cloves
confectioners' sugar

Eliane's cookies

spiced sesame rolls

2¼ cups white bread flour
½ tablespoon sea salt
⅔ teaspoon ground cumin
⅔ teaspoon ground coriander
¼ oz. fresh yeast or
  1½ teaspoons dried yeast
¼ teaspoon sugar
4 tablespoons sunflower oil
1 egg white, beaten
1½ tablespoons sesame seeds

In Egypt and other parts of the Middle East these rolls are made in a very small size and served with drinks.

1 Put the flour in a large bowl with the salt. Stir in the ground cumin and coriander. Crumble the yeast into a small bowl, adding the sugar and ⅝ cup warm water. Put both yeast and flour in a warm place for 10 minutes, then make a well in the center of the flour and pour in the yeast mixture. Cover the yeast with flour, then add the oil, mixing with a wooden spoon. Stir hard until the dough clings together, then turn out on a floured surface and knead briefly. Clean the bowl and rub with oil, then replace the dough, cover with a cloth and leave in a warm place for about 1½ hours or until doubled in volume.

2 Punch down the dough and knead again for 1–2 minutes. Then divide into small balls; roll them out into thin sausage shapes about 4 inches long and as thick as your little finger. Form them into a circle and pinch the ends together, dampening them with a drop of water. Lay them on oiled baking sheets and put back in a warm place for about 12 minutes, until starting to rise. Then brush them with beaten egg white and sprinkle with sesame seeds. Bake in a preheated oven, 350°F, for 30 minutes, then turn off the heat and leave them in the cooling oven for another 10 minutes. They are best served the same day, but can be kept for 1–2 days in an airtight container.

Makes about 24

chutneys, relishes, and accompaniments

Preserved limes are especially good eaten with chicken or vegetarian curries, or rice dishes. To make, wash and thinly slice 10 large limes. Deseed 4 red chilies and then cut in thin strips. Peel and finely chop 1 oz. fresh root ginger. Lay the sliced limes in a wide-mouthed jar, scattering chili, ginger, and a total of 2 teaspoons dried lemon grass between the layers. When all are used up, pour over the juice of 8–10 Seville oranges or 4 large oranges and 2 lemons. There should be enough juice to come level with the limes. Close the jar tightly and leave for 10 days before eating, shaking the jar every day. Once opened, this must be kept in the refrigerator.

red curry paste

Different in color and in character from the "fresh" Green Curry Paste (see below), this curry paste is based on dried red chilies and is quite strong. It is best suited to use in meat curries.

1 Toast the coriander, cumin, and caraway seeds and peppercorns in a heavy skillet over gentle heat for 1–2 minutes. Leave to cool for a few minutes, then pour into a small electric mill and grind to a powder. Turn into a bowl.

2 Put the chopped chilies, lemon grass, shallots, garlic, and lime rind into the mill in batches and grind. Add all the dry ingredients to the bowl and mix. Add the salt, then stir in the vegetable oil to make a fairly smooth paste. Spoon into a small jar and close tightly. It will keep for 6–8 weeks under refrigeration.

Makes about 5 oz., enough for about 4 curries.

- **1 tablespoon coriander seeds**
- **½ tablespoon cumin seeds**
- **1 teaspoon caraway seeds**
- **10 black peppercorns**
- **10 dried red chilies, deseeded and chopped**
- **2 stalks lemon grass, peeled and finely chopped**
- **3 shallots, chopped**
- **3 garlic cloves, chopped**
- **rind of 1 lime, chopped**
- **2 teaspoons sea salt**
- **3–4 tablespoons vegetable oil**

green curry paste

In Thailand curries are made mostly with pastes made from a complex combination of fresh and dried herbs and freshly ground spices. This green curry paste uses large quantities of green chilies, fresh lemon grass, and limes, and is especially suited to fish and chicken dishes.

Put the coriander and caraway seeds and black peppercorns in a mortar and pound until crushed, or use an electric spice mill or coffee mill. Transfer the crushed spices to a food processor with all the other ingredients and process to a rough paste. Pack into a screw-top jar and store in the refrigerator. It can be kept for 4–6 weeks under refrigeration and used as needed.

Makes about 3½ oz., enough for about 4 curries.

- **1 teaspoon coriander seeds**
- **1 teaspoon caraway seeds**
- **10 black peppercorns**
- **½ teaspoon ground nutmeg**
- **½ teaspoon ground cloves**
- **10 large green chilies, deseeded and chopped**
- **2 tablespoons chopped shallots**
- **2 tablespoons chopped garlic**
- **1 tablespoon grated galangal or fresh root ginger**
- **2 stalks lemon grass, crushed and chopped**
- **rind of 2 lemons, chopped**
- **2 teaspoons sea salt**
- **4 tablespoons sunflower oil**

coconut milk

Coconut milk does not include any spices; indeed, it is the most bland and soothing of foods. For this very reason it is a vital ingredient of many highly spiced dishes. Southeast Asian curries of fish, chicken, and meat almost always include coconut milk, and it is this that gives them much of their appeal. Ceviche of raw fish is made with coconut milk on the island of Fiji, as is an unusual ice cream. Since the process is lengthy and requires detailed explanations, I have chosen to give it here, for easy reference.

Fresh coconuts can now be bought at any time of the year. Shake them before buying to make sure you can hear liquid sloshing around inside; this proves they are fresh. Each coconut will yield 10–12 oz. flesh.

To open the coconut, first pierce holes in 2 of the 3 "eyes" with a hammer and screwdriver or strong skewer, and drain off the liquid. This liquid is not much use in cooking, but makes a refreshing drink. Place the nut in a preheated oven, 375°F, for 20–25 minutes, by which time the shell will have cracked. Lay the nut on a hard surface, preferably a stone floor or doorstep, and tap it sharply all around the middle with a hammer. Then hit it hard; the shell should then fall away, leaving the brown-lined flesh separate but fairly intact. Pare away the brown skin with a vegetable peeler, then cut the flesh in 1 inch pieces and chop finely in a food processor. If only a small amount of grated coconut is needed, the brown skin may be left on and the flesh grated by hand, or the whole amount may be processed as above and the surplus frozen.

To make coconut milk from fresh coconut:

Put the grated flesh of 1 coconut, about 10 oz., in a food processor and cover with 3 cups almost-boiling water. Let stand for 4 minutes, then process for 1 minute and pour through a strainer lined with cheesecloth, squeezing the cloth to extract every drop of liquid. This will yield about 2½ cups medium-thick coconut milk. If more is needed, a second, thinner batch can be obtained by repeating the process with the same batch of grated coconut and 1⅞ cups hot water. Coconut milk will keep for up to 2 days in the refrigerator.

To make coconut milk from packaged, unsweetened dried coconut:

Put 6 oz. dried coconut in a food processor with 2½ cups hot water. Let stand for 3 minutes, then process for 1 minute. Strain as for fresh grated coconut milk, above. This will yield about 2 cups. A second, thinner batch can be obtained by repeating the process with the same coconut and 1⅞ cups hot water. The two batches can then be mixed together.

To make coconut milk from creamed coconut:

Chop 7 oz. creamed coconut and put in a blender or food processor with 1½ cups hot water. Process for a few moments, then leave to cool. This makes 2½ cups fairly thick coconut milk, which can be diluted as required.
Note: Canned coconut milk can be bought in Asian markets, as can powdered coconut milk, which should be used according to the directions on the package. Both vary according to the brand, but are usually satisfactory.

chilies in oil

A useful way of preserving small chilies is to immerse them in oil, which can itself be used as a flavoring agent for sprinkling — sparingly — over pizzas and other dishes. Since one rarely wants more than 1 or 2 chilies at a time, and they do not keep indefinitely, this is both practical and economical. Both fresh and dried chilies can be used in this way. (The only point of using dried chilies, which have already been preserved by the drying process, is to flavor the oil.)

Wash and dry the chilies. Trim the stalks. Pack upright into a jar with a tightly fitting lid. Pour over enough olive oil to cover completely. Close the lid tightly. The chilies will keep for months, and the oil can be replenished as it is used. The chilies must always remain covered.

peppered almonds

Always buy unskinned almonds and skin them yourself; after a few tries you will have learned the knack and be able to do it quite quickly. I like to use the Southwest-style chili powder (sometimes called chile*) for this, since its other ingredients (cumin, oregano, and garlic) add interest, but this is not vital.*

¾ cup almonds, unskinned

1 tablespoon butter

½ tablespoon sea salt

⅛–¼ teaspoon *chile*, chili powder, or cayenne

1 Put the almonds in a small bowl and cover them with boiling water. Let them stand for 3–4 minutes, then lift out a few at a time. The skins should slip off quite easily; if not, put the nuts back in the hot water for a few more minutes. As the water cools, drain it away and cover the remaining almonds with more boiling water. The whole process will get easier as you progress, until you can do it with one hand, like Audrey Hepburn breaking eggs in *Sabrina*.

2 When all the almonds are skinned, dry them well in a cloth. Heat the butter in a skillet. When it is very hot but not yet smoking, put in the almonds and fry them quite quickly, turning with a spatula, until straw-colored. This will take about 2 minutes. Drain the nuts on paper towels, then put them in a dish. Mix the sea salt and the *chile*, chili powder or cayenne in a small bowl. (If the salt is in large crystals, it may be quickly run through a small electric spice mill or coffee mill with the spice.) Scatter the mixture over the hot almonds and mix together well. Peppered almonds are best eaten the same day as made, still warm if possible, although they can be kept for 1–2 days in an airtight container.

Serves 6 with drinks before a meal.

apple relish

This is a simple relish to make with ingredients that are usually on hand. The chili pow-der may be omitted if the relish is to accompany a very hot dish.

Beat the yogurt until smooth, then stir in the other ingredients, using the chili powder or not, as preferred. Chill for a little while before serving.

Serves 4 with curry-style dishes or lentil dhals.

⅝ cup yogurt
1 hard green dessert apple, such as
   Granny Smith, unpeeled and
   coarsely grated
¼ teaspoon chili powder (optional)
2 teaspoons lemon juice
1 tablespoon chopped fresh mint

cucumber raita

This is a classic Indian recipe, very similar to the Greek tzatziki, usually made without spices as a bland, cooling accompaniment to hot dishes. But I cannot bear to make it without Madhur Jaffrey's addition of toasted and ground cumin seeds, which adds subtlety. The Greeks use no spices but lots of garlic, and dried mint instead of fresh.

1 If including cumin, toast it in advance in a dry skillet over a gentle heat for 1–2 minutes, shaking the pan frequently. As soon as the seeds start to change color, remove from the heat. Allow to cool for a few minutes, then grind in a coffee mill or small blender.
2 Put the yogurt into a bowl and beat with a whisk until smooth. Squeeze out excess moisture from the grated cucumber, then stir into the yogurt. Add the cumin, if using, the chopped mint, and sea salt and black pepper to taste. Chill until ready to serve, with curries, grilled meat, or roast lamb.

Makes about 1¼ cups

½ teaspoon cumin seeds (optional)
1¼ cups thick yogurt
¼ large cucumber, peeled and very
   coarsely grated
1½ tablespoons chopped mint
sea salt and black pepper

ginger butter

An unusual preserve, excellent with grilled fish or meat, it can be eaten soon after making or frozen for future use.

1 Put the butter in a food processor and add the grated ginger. Crush the garlic cloves into the butter and add the lemon juice and cilantro, if using, and sea salt and black pepper. Process until smoothly blended and then chill for about 30 minutes to firm.

2 Divide in half and form each piece into a roll. Wrap in foil to freeze. To serve, simply cut the roll into slices about ½ inch thick. Lay a slice over a broiled sirloin steak, broiled Dover sole, or freshly cooked noodles.

Serves 8

1 cup butter, cut in pieces
2 oz. fresh root ginger, peeled and grated
2 garlic cloves, peeled
2 tablespoons lemon juice
1 tablespoon finely chopped cilantro leaves (optional)
sea salt and black pepper

pickled grapes

This is a Turkish preserve, perfect for eating in hot, sultry weather.

Divide half the grapes into small bunches and pack them into wide-mouthed preserving jars, scattering the mustard seeds among them. Press the remaining grapes, strain the juice, and measure it. Add an equal amount of white wine vinegar, bring it to a boil, and pour over the grapes. Leave to cool, then close the jars tightly and keep for 4 weeks before eating.

Fills 4 x 1 lb. preserving jars.

4 lb. small green seedless grapes
2 tablespoons white mustard seeds
about 2½ cups white wine vinegar

mango relish

Put the chopped mangoes in a bowl and stir in the sliced scallions, chopped chili, grated ginger, lime juice, chopped cilantro leaves, sea salt, and black pepper. Chop very roughly with a hand-held blender. Serve at room temperature with curries.

Serves 4

2 mangoes, slightly under-ripe, peeled and chopped

5 scallions, bulbs only, sliced

1 green chili, deseeded and finely chopped

2 inch square piece fresh root ginger, peeled and grated

4 tablespoons lime juice

2 tablespoons chopped fresh cilantro leaves

sea salt and black pepper

pickled kumquats

Make this in the autumn to eat with cold meat and game.

1 Put the kumquats in a pan and cover with water. Bring to a boil and cook steadily for about 35 minutes or until they are soft when pierced with a skewer. Drain them.

2 Put the sugar in a clean pan and add the vinegar and spices. Bring to a boil and cook gently until the sugar has melted. Then put in the drained kumquats and bring back to a boil. Simmer gently for 15 minutes, then let stand overnight.

3 Next day, bring back to a boil and simmer for another 15 minutes. Then remove from the heat, and lift out the fruit with a slotted spoon and pack it into glass preserving jars. Boil the syrup until it has reduced somewhat, just enough to cover the kumquats and fill the jars. Pour it over them and screw down the lids tightly. Keep for 1 month before eating, if you can bear to. It is excellent with cold ham, game, and turkey.

Note: Because the kumquats have been pickled in pure vinegar, the jars do not need to be sterilized and sealed as for bottled fruit in syrup. An airtight seal is all that is needed; otherwise the vinegar will evaporate.

Makes enough to fill approximately 2 x 1 lb. preserving jars.

1 lb. kumquats
2 cups sugar
1⅞ cups red or white wine
  vinegar
2 inch stick cinnamon
6 cloves

spiced plum sauce

This is a useful sauce, rather like a fresh preserve, best made in autumn for eating with hot or cold game, cold meat, game pie, goose, duck, and all sorts of terrine. It will keep, tightly sealed and refrigerated, for 2–3 weeks.

1½ lb. plums, pitted and roughly
   chopped
1¼ cups red wine
4 tablespoons brandy
juice and rind of 2 oranges
juice and rind of 2 lemons
2 inch cinnamon stick
6 cloves
6 tablespoons redcurrant jelly
2 tablespoons Dijon mustard

1 Put the chopped plums in a pan with the red wine and brandy. Add the rind of both oranges and 1 lemon, cut in thin strips, and the cinnamon and cloves. Bring to a boil and simmer for 10 minutes, covered. Put the redcurrant jelly in a small bowl, stand it in a pan of very hot water, and melt it. (Commercially made jelly will probably need to be strained after melting.) Add the mustard and stir until blended, then add 4 tablespoons each of orange and lemon juice.

2 Discard the cinnamon and cloves, and put the cooked plums with their juice in a blender. Add the fruit juices and the jelly and mustard mixture. Blend briefly, stopping before it is completely smooth. Serve the same day as making, at room temperature, or store in glass preserving jars, tightly closed and refrigerated.

Makes 4¼ cups

tamarind syrup

This Turkish delicacy makes a useful preserve for adding to sweet and sour dishes such as curries of fish or chicken, or to desserts such as spiced fruit salads, or even to homemade lemonade. Tamarind is usually bought compressed into a solid block. Much easier to use, but not often available, is a thick purée looking rather like jam, sold in jars. Indian and Thai stores are the best sources. There is little point in using the purée to make syrup, as it is already easy to use, while the block poses problems.

6 oz. compressed tamarind, in block
   form
1½ cups sugar

1 Pull the compressed tamarind apart into small pieces and put it in a pan with 5 cups water. Bring it to a boil and boil steadily until reduced by half (about 20 minutes), then strain into a clean pan and add the sugar. Cook for 2–3 minutes, just until the sugar has dissolved, then remove from the heat and leave to cool.

2 Pour into a strainer and leave to drip into a bowl. You should have about 2½ cups of beautiful clear pink syrup, with an exquisite taste. Pour into a wide-mouthed jar and close tightly. Once opened, keep refrigerated.

Makes about 2½ cups

tapenade

A typical Provençal dish, full of strong flavors and spices merged into an oily paste, tapenade can be eaten on slices of French bread as a first course or with drinks.

3 oz. anchovy fillets

2 tablespoons milk

1½ cups black olives, pitted

1 cup capers, drained

3 oz. canned tuna fish, drained

1 tablespoon mustard powder

1 cup olive oil

2 tablespoons brandy

½ teaspoon ground allspice

¼ teaspoon ground black pepper

1 Soak the anchovy fillets in the milk for 10 minutes, then drain. Put them in a food processor with the olives, capers, tuna fish, and mustard. Process to a smooth paste, then turn into a bowl and stir in the olive oil very gradually, as if making mayonnaise.

2 Lastly stir in the brandy and spices — salt will not be needed. Spoon into a small dish and chill. Serve with slices of French bread dried in the oven, or with toasted pita bread, as a first course or as a snack with drinks. This useful paste can be made in advance and kept in the refrigerator, well-covered, for 2–3 weeks.

Serves 4 to 6 as a first course, or 8 with drinks.

West Indian seasoning

1 onion, grated

2 garlic cloves, crushed

½ teaspoon ground nutmeg

½ teaspoon ground cloves

½ teaspoon curry powder

2 teaspoons fresh thyme or
  1 teaspoon dried thyme

2 teaspoons chopped fresh marjo-
  ram or 1 teaspoon dried marjoram

1 tablespoon sea salt

2 teaspoons finely chopped chives

2–3 dashes Tabasco sauce

4 tablespoons lime juice

This comes from Barbados, where it is used to season chicken and fish before frying.

Mix all the ingredients together in a bowl and use to rub on chicken or fish before frying or grilling (see Caribbean Fried Chicken, page 120).

Makes about 1 cup

Purée fresh raspberries, sweeten lightly, and mix with yogurt. Sprinkle with freshly ground black pepper for a delicious summer dessert.

desserts

ginger apple crumble

2 lb. cooking apples, peeled, cored,
  and coarsely chopped
4 tablespoons sugar
2 tablespoons lemon juice
2 tablespoons water

Crumble:
I cup cake flour, sifted
¼ teaspoon salt
⅓ cup butter, diced
¼ cup light brown sugar
2 teaspoons ground ginger

1 Butter a dish holding about 2 pints. Put the chopped apples into it, adding the sugar, lemon juice, and water.

2 Mix the crumble in a food processor or by hand. If using a processor, put the flour, salt, and diced butter in first and process until it resembles fine breadcrumbs, then add the sugar and ginger and process again. If making by hand, sift the flour and salt into a large bowl and cut in the butter as if making pastry. Finally, mix in the sugar and ginger with the blade of a knife.

3 Pile the crumble on top of the apples, smoothing the surface with a palette knife, and bake in a preheated oven, 350°F, for 40 minutes, until golden brown. Serve within the hour, warm rather than hot. Delicious accompaniments are Vanilla Custard Sauce (see page 195), Ginger or Vanilla Ice Cream (see pages 235 and 243), or simply a pitcher of thick cream.

Serves 4 to 6

baked ginger custard
with kiwi fruit

3 oz. fresh root ginger, peeled
3 egg yolks, beaten
2½ tablespoons sugar
1¼ cups light cream
1¼ cups heavy cream
6 kiwi fruit, cut in half lengthwise and
  sliced in semi-circles, to garnish

1 Crush the peeled ginger in a garlic press to extract 2 teaspoons juice. Beat the egg yolks with the sugar and add the ginger juice. Heat the light and heavy creams almost to boiling point, and then pour onto the egg yolks. Mix well, then pour through a strainer into 6 small *oeuf en cocotte* dishes or ramekins.

2 Stand them in a baking pan half full of hot water and bake in a preheated oven, 300°F, for 35 minutes or until they are just set. Cool, then chill for several hours or overnight. Turn out onto flat platter to serve, surrounded by sliced kiwi fruit.

Serves 6

ginger apple ring

Ground ginger and apple make a good combination, especially when served with a sauce (see below) or thick cream.

1 Make the apple purée first. Put the apples in a heavy pan with just enough water to cover the bottom. Add the sugar and bring slowly to a boil. Cook gently until the apples are soft, stirring occasionally, then push through a medium food mill. Do not strain, mill finely, or blend in a processor, as the purée should not be too smooth.

2 Butter a ring mold holding roughly 3 cups. Then make the ginger mixture. Sift the flour into a large bowl with the baking soda, baking powder, spices, and salt. Stir in the lightly beaten egg. Warm the syrup, molasses, sugar, and butter together until the butter has melted; do not overheat. Stir into the flour with just enough milk to make a thin mixture that can be poured. Pour into the ring mold and bake in a preheated oven, 350°F, for 30 minutes or until firm and lightly colored, and coming away from the edges. Turn out on to a wire rack to cool for 15–20 minutes before serving, then transfer to a flat dish and fill the center with the stewed apples. The apples may be warm or at room temperature, but not chilled. Serve with Vanilla Custard Sauce (see page 195) with some thick cream incorporated, with Ginger Sauce (see page 194), or with a pitcher of thick cream.

Serves 6

Apple purée:
2 lb. apples, peeled, cored, and cut in eighths
4 tablespoons sugar

Ginger mixture:
1¼ cups cake flour
½ teaspoon baking soda
½ teaspoon baking powder
¾ teaspoon ground ginger
¼ teaspoon ground allspice
¼ teaspoon ground cinnamon
a pinch of salt
1 egg, lightly beaten
3 tablespoons golden syrup
3 tablespoons dark molasses
3 tablespoons dark brown or muscovado sugar
⅓ cup butter, diced
1–2 tablespoons milk

apple tarts
with cinnamon ice cream

Cinnamon and apples are a delicious combination, and this dish is a perfect example of spice, fruit, and cream combined. If you do not have time to make the ice cream, some ground cinnamon may be added to the apples instead.

Pastry:
2¼ cups cake flour
½ teaspoon sugar
½ cup butter, diced
3–5 tablespoons iced water
1 egg yolk
1 tablespoon milk

Filling:
2–3 Granny Smith or other tart eating apples
3 tablespoons sugar
(1 teaspoon ground cinnamon if not serving with cinnamon ice cream)
2 tablespoons butter, diced
Cinnamon Ice Cream (see page 230), to serve

1 Both ice cream and pastry may be made up to 1 day in advance. To make the pastry, sift the flour and sugar into a food processor or large bowl, adding the butter. Process or cut in by hand until it resembles fine breadcrumbs. Then add the iced water gradually, processing or stirring by hand, until the dough clings together. Wrap in floured plastic wrap and chill for 20 minutes.

2 Butter 6 shallow tart pans measuring roughly ¾ x 4 inches. Divide the dough into 6 equal pieces and roll each one out to line a pan. Chill again, if time permits, for 10–20 minutes, then weigh down with foil and dried beans. Bake in a preheated oven, 375°F, for 5 minutes, then remove the foil and beans. Beat the egg yolk and milk together; brush the pastry cases with this and bake them for another 8 minutes. Leave to cool.

3 About 1–2 hours before serving, cut the apples in quarters, removing core and peel, and cut each quarter across into small chunky slices about ¼ inch thick. Lay them in the pastry cases and sprinkle 1½ teaspoons sugar over each one. (If not making the cinnamon ice cream, mix the ground cinnamon with the sugar before sprinkling over the apples.) Dot them with butter, then bake in a preheated oven, 400°F, for 10 minutes. Serve within the hour if possible, while still warm, with the cinnamon ice cream in a separate bowl.

Serves 6

cinnamon ice cream

This unusual ice cream is delicious served alone, or with apples served warm in the form of a pie, tart, or a simple compote.

1 Put the milk in a small pan with the cinnamon sticks and heat slowly, stopping just before it reaches boiling point. Cover the pan and then leave to infuse for 20–30 minutes.

2 Put the egg yolks into a bowl or the top part of a double boiler. If using a bowl, have a pan that fits it neatly half filled with simmering water, being careful that the water does not touch the base of the bowl. Beat the egg yolks, adding the sugar, until they are foamy and light in color. Then reheat the milk, remove the cinnamon sticks, and pour the milk slowly onto the egg yolks, beating constantly. Stand the bowl or top half of the double boiler over the simmering water and stir constantly. After 6–8 minutes the custard should thicken very slightly, just enough to make a thin coating on the back of the spoon. Remove the bowl or top half of the double boiler immediately and stand it in a sink half full of cold water. Stir now and then as the custard cools, to prevent a skin from forming. When it has reached room temperature, remove from the sink and fold in the lightly whipped cream. Now pour into an ice cream freezer and freeze, following the maker's instructions. Alternatively, pour into a metal container or ice trays with the dividers removed, cover with a lid or foil, and place in the freezer. Take out every hour or so and stir well, then replace. It may take 2–4 hours to freeze, depending on the temperature of the freezer and the type of container used.

3 Take out of the freezer about 30 minutes before serving, while eating the first course perhaps or when starting to serve the main course, depending on the type of meal.

Serves 4 alone, or 6 with an apple dish.

- 1¼ **cups milk**
- 3 x 1 **inch cinnamon sticks**
- 4 **egg yolks**
- 5 **tablespoons sugar**
- 1¼ **cups heavy or whipping cream, lightly whipped**

ginger pancakes
with fromage frais

For a simpler dish, these little pancakes are also very good served plain, without a filling, with cut lemons and sugar on the table.

1 First make the pancake batter. Sift the flour into a food processor with the salt, sugar and ground ginger, if using. Mix the milk with the water. Process the flour with the egg and egg yolk, adding the milk and water through the lid while continuing to process. Last of all, add the grated ginger, if using instead of ground ginger. (Alternatively, sift the flour, salt, sugar, and ground ginger, if using, into a large bowl and break the eggs into a well in the center. Beat with a hand-held electric mixer or a balloon whisk, adding the milk and water simultaneously, and then the grated ginger, if using.) When the batter is smooth, leave for 1–2 hours, if convenient.

2 For the filling, stir the chopped ginger into the *fromage frais*. Shortly before serving, process the batter or beat well by hand again and make the pancakes. Melt a tiny piece of butter in a non-stick skillet, heat it, then pour 1½ tablespoons batter into the pan and swirl it around to cover the entire surface. Cook for 1 minute on each side, turning once, and stack the cooked pancakes under a cloth to keep warm. When all are done, roll each one up around 1½ tablespoons of the ginger filling, with 5–6 raspberries, when available, laid on the filling. Lay the filled pancakes on a flat dish and scatter the remaining raspberries over and among them. Serve as soon as possible, while the pancakes are still warm.

Note: If it is not possible to make the pancakes at the last moment, make them in advance, let them cool before filling and serve the dish at room temperature.

Makes about 12 small (5 inch) pancakes; serves 6.

Pancakes:
1¼ cups cake flour
a pinch of salt
½ teaspoon sugar
1 teaspoon ground ginger, or peeled and grated fresh root ginger
⅓ cup milk
⅓ cup water
1 egg
1 egg yolk
1 teaspoon butter

Filling:
1½ oz. preserved ginger, chopped
1 cup *fromage frais* (or substitute neufchâtel cheese)
2 cups raspberries, when available

ginger hats

These little ginger cakes used to be served cold at teatime in English country houses between the wars. I like to serve them hot as a dessert with a sauce (see below).

1 Butter small muffin pans, ones which hold about ½ cup. Sift the flours and spices into a large bowl, then mix in the brown sugar. Warm the molasses, syrup, and butter in a small pan. When the butter has just melted, stir the syrup mixture into the dry ingredients, then add the beaten eggs.

2 Turn into the muffin pans and bake in a preheated oven, 350°F, for 20–25 minutes. Serve the Ginger Hats about 20 minutes after taking out of the oven, with Ginger Sauce (see page 194), Vanilla Custard Sauce (see page 195), or lightly whipped cream.

Makes 6 to 8, depending on the size of the muffin pans; serves 6.

¾ **cup cake flour**

¾ **cup self-raising flour**

½ **tablespoon ground ginger**

¼ **teaspoon ground allspice**

½ **cup soft brown sugar**

4 tablespoons molasses

4 tablespoons golden syrup, if available, or substitute 1 part dark corn syrup and 5 parts light corn syrup

½ **cup butter**

2 eggs, beaten

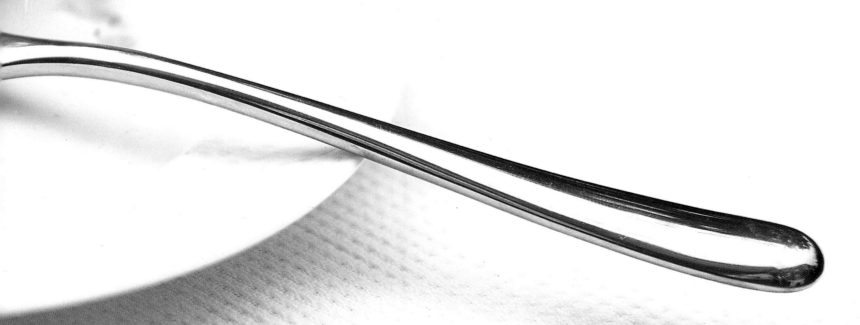

steamed ginger pudding

1 Oil a bowl holding approximately 1½ pints. Sift the flour into a separate large bowl with the salt, baking soda, and ginger. Mix in the suet and the breadcrumbs. Warm the syrup and molasses and stir them into the lightly beaten eggs. Stir this into the flour mixture, then turn into the oiled bowl. The mixture must not fill the bowl by more than three-quarters.

2 Cover with greased foil, tie down and steam for 2½–3 hours. Turn out to serve, with Ginger Sauce (see page 194), or Vanilla Custard Sauce (see page 195).

Serves 6

- I cup cake flour, sifted
- a pinch of salt
- I teaspoon baking soda
- I teaspoon ground ginger
- ⅔ cup shredded suet
- I cup soft white breadcrumbs
- 6 tablespoons golden syrup, if available, or substitute I part dark corn syrup and 5 parts light corn syrup
- 6 tablespoons molasses
- 2 eggs, lightly beaten

Greek rice pudding

In Greece, a cold rice pudding called rizogalo is often eaten for breakfast. It is sometimes flavored with mastic (see page 44). Alternatively, ground cinnamon is used.

1 Wash the rice and soak it in ½ cup water. Bring the milk to a boil with the sugar, then stir in the rice with its water. Bring back to a boil and cook steadily for 40 minutes, covered, until most — but not all — the liquid has been absorbed. Stir the corn flour into 1 tablespoon water, then add to the rice and cook for another 5 minutes, stirring. Stir the egg yolk and milk mixture into the rice and cook over low heat for 2–3 minutes, stirring.

2 If using mastic as a flavoring, pound it in a mortar with a pinch of sugar and stir into the rice with the rose water. Simmer for 2 minutes, then pour into individual bowls and leave to cool. If using cinnamon instead of mastic, simply sprinkle it over the rice pudding in the serving bowls. Serve cold but not chilled.

Serves 4

- ¼ cup pudding rice
- 2½ cups milk
- 3 tablespoons vanilla sugar or granulated sugar
- 2 teaspoons corn flour
- I egg yolk beaten with I tablespoon milk

Flavorings (optional):
- I piece mastic about the size of a pellet of chewing gum
- a pinch of sugar
- 2 teaspoons rose water
- *or* ground cinnamon

cardamom rice pudding

Use some of the butter to grease a pie plate. Wash the rice and put it in the buttered plate. Scatter the sugar over it and pour the milk on top. Stir with a fork, then drop in the coarsely crushed cardamom pods. Scatter the rest of the butter over the surface of the plate and bake in a preheated oven, 250°F, for 2–2½ hours until light golden brown. Serve warm, about 30 minutes after taking out of the oven, with a pitcher of chilled light cream.

Serves 4

**1 tablespoon butter, cut in small
  pieces**
¼ cup rice
2 tablespoons sugar
2½ cups milk
2 cardamom pods, coarsely crushed

ginger ice cream

This is usually made with costly preserved stem ginger, but this version using inexpensive ground ginger is just as delicious.

1 Heat the milk in a small pan, adding the ground ginger. Beat the egg yolks, adding the sugar, until they are foamy and light in color, then add the hot milk gradually, beating constantly. Now stand the bowl, or the top half of a double boiler, over a pan of simmering water, making sure the water does not touch the bottom of the bowl. Stir constantly for 6–8 minutes or until the custard has thickened very slightly, just enough to coat the back of the spoon. When this has happened, remove immediately from the heat and stand the bowl or pan in a sink half full of cold water. Stir now and then to prevent a skin from forming.

2 As the custard cools, stir in the honey. When it has reached room temperature, fold in the lightly whipped cream. Now pour into an ice cream freezer and freeze, following the maker's instructions. Alternatively, pour into a shallow metal container or ice trays with the dividers removed, cover with a lid or foil, and place in the freezer. Take out every hour or so and stir well, then replace. It may take 2–4 hours to freeze, depending on the temperature of the freezer and the type of container used. If frozen solid, remove from the freezer about 30 minutes before serving. This wonderful ice cream may be served alone, with brandy snaps, or plain cookies, or with an apple or pear tart or compote.

Serves 4 to 6

1¼ cups milk
2 teaspoons ground ginger
4 egg yolks
2 tablespoons sugar
4 tablespoons clear honey
**1¼ cups heavy cream, lightly
  whipped**

spiced fruit salad

A friend and colleague, Sybil Kapoor, gave me this recipe, showing how spices can subtly enhance the flavor of fresh fruit. The choice of fruit can be altered to suit the time of year.

Spiced syrup:

1¼ cups water

½ cup sugar

juice and rind of 1 lemon

3 star anise

6 black peppercorns

6 whole cardamoms

1 vanilla pod

Salad:

4 ripe peaches, peeled and sliced

4 figs, each cut into 8

2 cups blueberries

1 Place the water, sugar, lemon rind, and spices in a saucepan over moderate heat. Dissolve the sugar before bringing the syrup to a boil. Simmer gently for 10 minutes, then remove from the heat. Add the lemon juice and leave to cool. The longer the spices are left in the syrup, the spicier the syrup will become.

2 Strain the syrup, or simply remove the rind, and pour the syrup, with or without the remaining spices, into a bowl. Add the sliced peaches, cut figs, and blueberries. Chill and serve with *crème fraîche*, if available (or substitute sour cream) or, even better, with Coconut Ice Cream (see page 241).

Note: Half the fun of spiced fruit salads is to alter the spices to taste. Coriander seeds can replace the star anise, while a small cinnamon stick can be used instead of the vanilla pod. Their subtle flavors can be further enhanced by substituting an orange for the lemon. When I have some already made, I often add 2–4 tablespoons Tamarind Syrup (see page 222) to the cooling spiced syrup.

Serves 4 on its own, or 6 with ice cream.

strawberries
with black pepper

An unusual but surprisingly good combination, especially when made with the juice of blood oranges, this makes a refreshing dessert at the end of a fairly elaborate dinner. It also makes a delicious breakfast, for those who like to avoid sweet dishes at the start of the day.

Lay the sliced strawberries on individual dishes or on a single flat dish. Pour the orange juice on top and grind a light sprinkling of black pepper over them.

Note: For a breakfast dish for 1 person, I allow 6 oz. strawberries.

Serves 4

1 lb. strawberries, hulled and thickly sliced

6 tablespoons freshly squeezed juice of blood oranges, when available, or ordinary oranges

black pepper

coffee cardamom ice cream

The pairing of cardamom with coffee is a reminder of the Middle East, where a crushed cardamom pod is often added to the coffee beans.

1 Make the coffee by your usual method, but using twice as much coffee as usual; then dissolve the instant coffee in it. Put the milk in a small pan with the crushed cardamom; bring slowly to a boil, then cover the pan, remove from the heat, and let stand for 20 minutes. Then remove the cardamom, add the coffee to the pan and reheat the coffee and milk together.

2 Beat the egg yolks, adding the sugar gradually, until they are foamy and light in color. Then reheat the coffee and cardamom mixture and pour it slowly into the egg yolks, beating constantly. Stand the bowl over a pan of simmering water, making sure that the water does not touch the bottom of the bowl, or use a double boiler. Stir constantly for 6–8 minutes or until the mixture has thickened just enough to coat the back of a wooden spoon. Remove the bowl or top half of the double boiler and let it stand in a sink half full of cold water. Stir now and then as it cools to room temperature, to prevent a skin from forming.

3 Remove the bowl from the sink and fold in the lightly whipped cream. Pour the mixture into an ice cream freezer and freeze, following the maker's instructions. Alternatively, pour the mixture into a shallow metal container or ice trays with the dividers removed, cover with a lid or foil, and place in the freezer. Take out every hour or so and stir well, then replace. It may take 2–4 hours to freeze, depending on the temperature of the freezer and the type of container used. If frozen solid, remove from the freezer about 30 minutes before serving.

Note: For a special occasion, this is delicious served with two other ice creams: Vanilla (see page 243), and chocolate.

Serves 4, or 6 with another dish.

⅝ cup black coffee, made double strength

2 teaspoons best-quality instant coffee granules

⅝ cup milk

1 cardamom pod, lightly crushed

4 egg yolks

⅓ cup sugar

1¼ cups heavy cream, lightly whipped

coconut ice cream

This unusual ice cream is best made with thin coconut milk derived from fresh or dried coconut, or from powdered coconut; canned coconut milk is too thick. The garnish of toasted coconut comes from Ices, the Definitive Guide *by Caroline Liddell and Robin Weir, with the authors' kind permission (Hodder and Stoughton, 1993).*

1 fresh coconut

4 egg yolks

⅓ cup vanilla sugar or granulated sugar

1¼ cups heavy cream

1¼ cups thin coconut milk

1 Open the coconut as directed for making Coconut Milk (see page 215). Extract the white flesh and remove the brown lining with a potato peeler. Grate the flesh or chop it finely in a food processor or blender. Weigh 5 oz. and set aside. Make thin coconut milk with the rest of the grated or chopped coconut by covering with 1⅞ cups almost-boiling water and leaving for 4 minutes. Pour into a food processor and process for 1 minute, then pour through a strainer lined with cheesecloth and squeeze until every last drop is extracted. Alternatively, use powdered coconut milk.

2 To make the ice cream, beat the egg yolks with the sugar. Heat the cream almost to boiling point, then pour into the egg yolks, continuing to beat. Stand the bowl over a pan of simmering water and stir with a wooden spoon for about 7 minutes, until the mixture has thickened slightly, just enough to coat the back of the spoon. Then remove from the heat and stir in the coconut milk. Reserve 2 tablespoons of the grated or chopped coconut and stir the rest into the mixture. Now pour into an ice cream freezer and freeze, following the maker's instructions. Alternatively, pour into a metal container or ice trays with the dividers removed, cover with a lid or foil, and place in the freezer. Take out every hour or so and stir well, then replace. It may take 2–4 hours to freeze, depending on the temperature of the freezer and the type of container used.

3 If frozen solid, remove the ice cream from the freezer about 30 minutes before serving. At the same time spread the reserved coconut on a cookie sheet and toast in a preheated oven, 325°F, for 10 minutes, until light golden brown. Cool and reserve. To serve, spoon the ice cream into a glass or china bowl and scatter the toasted coconut over the surface. Serve alone or with Spiced Fruit Salad (see page 237).

Serves 4 to 6

seven-cup pudding
with vanilla custard sauce

This is an old-fashioned Scottish pudding, less rich than a Christmas pudding but highly spiced. It is best made using a teacup holding 6 fl. oz. (¾ cup) to measure the major ingredients rather than weighing them.

1 Mix the dry ingredients except for the baking soda in a large bowl. Break the egg into a large measuring cup and make up to ¾ cup with milk. Beat together, then stir into the dry ingredients. Dissolve the baking soda in the wine vinegar for 3 minutes, then stir into the pudding mixture.

2 Butter a pudding bowl holding approximately 3 pints and pour in the mixture. The mixture should not fill the bowl by more than three-quarters. Cover with greased foil, tie down and steam for 4 hours. About 1 hour before serving, make the Vanilla Custard Sauce (see page 195), with or without cream. Turn out the pudding to serve, with the warm sauce in a pitcher or sauceboat.

Serves 6 to 8

1 teacup soft white breadcrumbs
1 teacup shredded suet
1 teacup sultanas or white raisins
1 teacup currants
1 teacup sugar
1 teacup cake flour, sifted
½ cup chopped mixed peel
½ cup almonds, blanched and coarsely chopped
2 teaspoons ground ginger
1 teaspoon ground cinnamon
1 teaspoon ground allspice
a pinch of sea salt
1 egg
about ⅝ cup milk
1 teaspoon baking soda
1 teaspoon red or white wine vinegar
Vanilla Custard Sauce (see page 195), to serve

spiced curd cheese

1 Turn the yogurt into a strainer lined with cheesecloth, standing over a bowl. Tie the corners of the cloth together to form a bag, then suspend it over the sink, hanging from the tap, or over a bowl, hanging from the seat of a cane chair. Leave for 5–6 hours or overnight.

2 Turn the drained yogurt into a bowl and stir in the scallions, chilies or hot red pepper flakes, chives, and sea salt. Stir in the olive oil gradually. Turn into a small dish to serve with other cheeses, or serve alone with crackers.

Note: This also makes a useful dip to serve with crudités or to spread on squares of rye bread, for serving with drinks, or at a picnic.

Makes 1 lb.

2 lb. thick yogurt (do not use low fat yogurt)
3 tablespoons chopped scallions
2 red or green chilies, deseeded and chopped, or ½ teaspoon hot red pepper flakes
3 tablespoons chopped chives
1 teaspoon sea salt
1½ tablespoons extra virgin olive oil

vanilla ice cream

Homemade Vanilla Ice Cream, preferably made with Jersey cream and flavored with vanilla pods, is one of the most delectable desserts, at its very best when served within a few hours of making. If it does not seem too extravagant, use two freshly bought vanilla pods, but one will do, especially if you have some homemade vanilla sugar.

1¼ **cups milk**

1–2 **vanilla pods, halved and split**

4 **egg yolks**

⅓ **cup vanilla sugar or granulated sugar**

1¼ **cups heavy cream, lightly whipped**

1 Put the milk in a small pan; scrape the seeds out of the split pods into the milk, then add the pods. Heat slowly, stopping just before it reaches boiling point. Cover the pan and leave to infuse for 20–30 minutes.

2 Put the egg yolks into a bowl or the top part of a double boiler. If using a bowl, have a pan that fits it neatly half filled with simmering water, being careful that the water does not touch the base of the bowl. Beat the egg yolks, adding the sugar, until they are foamy and light in color. Then reheat the milk, remove the vanilla pods, and pour the milk slowly into the egg yolks, beating constantly. Stand the bowl or top half of the double boiler over the simmering water and stir constantly. After 6–8 minutes the custard should thicken very slightly, just enough to make a thin coating on the back of the spoon. Remove the bowl or top half of the double boiler immediately and stand it in a sink half full of cold water. Stir now and then as the custard cools, to prevent a skin from forming. When it has reached room temperature, remove from the sink and fold in the lightly whipped cream. Now pour into an ice cream freezer and freeze, following the maker's instructions. Alternatively, pour into a metal container or ice trays with the dividers removed, cover with a lid or foil, and place in the freezer. Take out every hour or so and stir well, then replace. It may take 2–4 hours to freeze, depending on the temperature of the freezer and the type of container used.

3 This is best served before it has frozen solid, but it may be hard to time exactly the first time you make it. If frozen solid, remove it from the freezer about 30 minutes before serving.

Serves 4 alone, or 6 as an accompaniment to another dish.

drinks

Although made with vodka, this is not a drink. It is simply a useful and economical way of making your own vanilla essence. Cut a fresh vanilla pod in half, then split each half in 2 pieces. Push them into a small glass bottle and fill up with vodka. Seal tightly, and store in a dark place for 2 weeks before using, to flavor fish sauces, or to pour over Aniseed or Vanilla Ice Cream (see page 243).

cardamom coffee

In the Arab countries of the Middle East the coffee is often flavored with cardamom. This gives it a wonderfully exotic aroma, transforming the character of the coffee into something strange and redolent of the East. The coffee must be ground extra fine, almost pulverized; ask for Turkish grind. The desired degree of sweetness must be determined beforehand, as the sugar is added in the making. A semi-sweet blend is probably popular with most people. Turkish coffee pots in thin metal are easily bought nowadays, and are quite inexpensive. Very small cups are also needed.

Put ⅜ cup water for each person into a Turkish pot. Add the sugar and bring to a boil. Add the coffee and cardamom pod(s), stir and bring back to a boil. When the froth rises to the top of the pot, remove the pot from the heat and allow the froth to sink. Then boil again and remove once more when the froth reaches the top. Put back over the heat for the third time, then, as the froth rises, pour the coffee immediately into little cups. Do this by degrees, so that some of the foam falls into each of the cups. Leave for a few moments before drinking, to allow the grounds to sink to the bottom. The coffee should not be stirred, so do not provide teaspoons; nor should the cups be drained.

1 heaped teaspoon sugar per person
½ tablespoon extra fine coffee per person
1–2 cardamom pods, lightly crushed (allow 1 cardamom pod for 2–3 servings)

eggnog

This is a delicious modern version of the ultra-rich, cholesterol-laden drink that used to be served at hunt breakfasts and other festive occasions. I often have one before going out in the evening to a theater or film, as I find it both festive and sustaining.

Put the milk in the blender or food processor with the beaten egg, sugar, spirits, and cracked ice. Blend or process at full speed until foamy and well mixed. Pour through a strainer into short, squat tumblers. Sprinkle freshly grated nutmeg generously over each one.

Serves 2 to 3

⅜ **cup milk**

I egg, beaten

2 teaspoons sugar

2–3 tablespoons bourbon, brandy, or rum

6 large ice cubes, cracked

freshly grated nutmeg, to garnish

lassi

This cooling yogurt drink is widely consumed in India, where it is sometimes flavored with toasted cumin seeds. The yogurt should be a fairly strong-tasting one or the drink will be very bland. An organic yogurt made with full-cream milk, not low-fat, is probably best, or a Greek yogurt.

1 Toast the cumin seeds, holding them over a low heat in a large metal spoon or soup ladle for about 1 minute. Then turn them into a mortar or small spice mill and grind.

2 Put the yogurt in a blender or food processor, add the iced water and blend, or beat with a hand-held electric beater or a balloon whisk, adding the cumin and sea salt to taste. Serve chilled, in tall glasses.

Serves 2 to 3

½ **teaspoon cumin seeds**

2½ **cups strong yogurt**

about 1¼ cups iced water

sea salt, to taste

pepper vodka

Russian and Polish vodkas are often flavored with different herbs, spices and fruit. This is one of the most unforgettable, with the contrast between the heat of the chilies and the icy chill of the vodka, served just above freezing point. The recipe is simplicity itself.

1 bottle superlative vodka, such as Absolut or Stolichnaya

3–5 small chilies, red and green mixed

10 juniper berries, very lightly crushed

1 Open the vodka bottle, slip in the chilies and the juniper berries and close tightly. Leave for 2–3 weeks before drinking.

2 If you have a freezer deep enough to hold the vodka bottle upright, you can create a spectacular effect by standing the bottle in a container slightly larger than itself filled with water. When the water has frozen solid, slip off the container by immersing briefly in warm water. Replace the vodka bottle, in its ice coat, in the freezer. The vodka itself will not freeze, because of its high alcohol content; it will simply become slightly syrupy and all the more delicious.

Makes 3–4⅜ cups, depending on the size of the bottle.

tamarind drink (jal jeera)

This is a delicious, slightly salty, cooling drink, pale and cloudy, flecked with green. The one made with tamarind purée is more authentic, but I prefer my own slightly sweet version, made with tamarind syrup.

Put all the ingredients in a blender or food processor together with 1 pint (600 ml) water. (If using tamarind purée, blend the purée first with 2 tablespoons water in a small mill before then adding the mixture to the blender or processor.) Process the whole thing until smoothly blended. Serve chilled or at room temperature, in tall glasses.

Serves 2 to 3

½ **tablespoon cumin seeds, roasted and ground**
1 **tablespoon Tamarind Purée (see page 50) or 4–6 tablespoons Tamarind Syrup (see page 222)**
¼ **teaspoon sea salt or ½ teaspoon if using syrup**
1 **tablespoon chopped fresh mint**
1 **tablespoon lime or lemon juice if using syrup**

mulled wine

Put the lemon and orange rinds, cloves, cinnamon, nutmeg, and sugar in a pan with 1¼ cups water. Bring slowly to a boil and cook gently until the sugar has melted. Then add the wine and bring back almost to boiling point. Remove from the heat, add the brandy, if using, and strain into a warmed glass pitcher. Serve hot.

Makes 4⅜ cups

rind of I lemon
rind of I orange
6 cloves
I cinnamon stick
½ nutmeg
3 tablespoons sugar
I½ bottles red wine
4–6 tablespoons brandy (optional)

fruit punch

The old-fashioned blender is best of all for making these sorts of delicious concoctions, but a food processor does the job adequately.

Put all the prepared fruit in the blender or processor with the orange juice or skimmed milk, roughly broken ice cubes, and tamarind syrup, if you have any already made. Process at high speed until well blended and foamy. Pour into short tumblers or glass bowls and serve at once.

Note: This is almost too thick to drink, and you may prefer to eat it with a spoon. Whichever way you drink or eat it, it is utterly delicious.

Serves 3

Illustrated on page 248

I lb. mixed fruit, weighed after preparing: bananas, melon, peaches, nectarines, plums, grapes and berries of all sorts; skinned, pitted, and cut in chunks
½ cup freshly squeezed orange juice or skimmed milk
3 ice cubes, broken
I tablespoon Tamarind Syrup (see page 222; optional)

index

Bold page numbers refer to entries in the spice directory and to spice mixtures.

Author's Acknowledgments

I should like to extend my sincere thanks to all the friends, relatives and colleagues who have helped me with this book, especially Suna Boyle, Christian Carritt, Vicky Cruickshank, Roz Denny, Soko Jope, Sybil Kapoor, Joumana Muir, Jill Norman, Rosemary Sayigh and Sri Owen. Also Darina Allen, whose day course on Indian spices at her Ballymaloe Cookery School, Midleton, Co. Cork, Ireland proved invaluable, and Dodie Miller, whose Cool Chile Co. (P.O. Box 5702, London W11 2GS), provided some fifteen different sorts of dried chilies, also a range of chili powders, together with recipe hints and suggestions, all by mail order.

Photographic Acknowledgments

Garden Picture Library/Lamontagne page 8
Nik Wheeler page 9

Notes

Standard level spoon measurements are used in all recipes.

Eggs should be medium unless otherwise stated.

Milk should be full fat unless otherwise stated.

Pepper should be freshly ground black pepper unless otherwise stated.

Fresh herbs should be used unless otherwise stated.

Ovens should be preheated to the specified temperature – if using a fan-assisted convection oven, follow the manufacturer's instructions for adjusting the time and the temperature.